The Two Germanys

The Dial Press
New York

THE TWO GERMANYS

JOHN DORNBERG

943.0387
Dor J

Library of Congress Cataloging in Publication Data
Dornberg, John. The two Germanys.
Summary: Traces the history of East and West Germany and
discusses the social, geographic, and political similarities
and differences of the two countries. Bibliography: p.   1. Germany—
Politics and government—Juvenile literature. 2. Germany (Federal
Republic, 1949–   )—Juvenile literature. 3. Germany (Democratic
Republic, 1949–   )—Juvenile literature. [1. Germany—Politics
and government. 2. Germany (Federal Republic, 1949–   )
3. Germany (Democratic Republic, 1949–   )] I. Title.
DD259.D66   914.3′03′87   73-15446
ISBN 0-8037-8757-x

Contents

a. 1

The Two Germanys

Germany? But where is it? I cannot find such a country.
Where the culture begins, the political realm ends.

Friedrich von Schiller
1759–1805

Germany will be either a world power or it will not
be at all.

Adolf Hitler
1889–1945

Introduction

For more than a quarter century after the end of World War II, when people spoke of Germany they generally meant only its western part, the Federal Republic, or FRG, whose capital, Bonn, is a small city on the banks of the Rhine River. This is the Germany that made most of the newspaper headlines—a country famed for its bug-shaped brand of automobiles, precision cameras, sausages, sauerkraut, and beer, for castles along the Rhine, cuckoo clocks in the Black Forest, onion-domed churches in Bavaria, smoke-billowing steel plants in the Ruhr. This is the Germany of the "economic miracle," that spectacular rise from the debris of war and Nazi dictatorship which made it one of the world's three greatest industrial and trading powers.

When people asked, "Where is Germany heading?" they

5

meant this Germany, linked closely by political, military, and commercial ties to the Western world. The faces of its postwar leaders such as Konrad Adenauer and Willy Brandt became almost as familiar to television viewers as those of American Presidents.

This is the part of Adolf Hitler's Third Reich that was occupied by the United States, Great Britain, and France after the Nazi regime's defeat on May 8, 1945. It is the Germany that claimed for itself, and was generally granted, the legacy of the old Reich: Its rights and obligations; its possessions and its debts; its fame and its infamy. It is a land of 62 million people who speak a variety of dialects. It comprises a territory of 96,000 square miles—about the size of Oregon. It is bordered by Czechoslovakia, Austria, Switzerland, France, Luxembourg, Belgium, Holland, the North Sea, Denmark, the Baltic Sea and—to the east—by a second Germany.

That other Germany—the eastern part—has about one-fourth as many inhabitants as the FRG: 17 million, and less than half as much territory: 41,000 square miles, an area comparable to that of Ohio. It is bordered on the south by Czechoslovakia, on the north by the Baltic Sea, and on the east by Silesia and Pomerania, two former provinces of the German Reich which now belong to Poland. Officially it is called the German Democratic Republic, or GDR.

Situated in its territory, about 120 miles from the West German border, is the city of Berlin, the former capital of the German Reich. Berlin's western sectors, with a population of 2.2 million, are still formally under American, British, and French occupation, though closely linked to the economic, political and cultural life of West Germany. The city's eastern part, although formally occupied by the Soviet Union, is the capital of the GDR.

6

THE TWO GERMANYS TODAY

This Germany, under Soviet occupation after the war, is a Communist country and is tied as closely to the Communist world as West Germany is to the West.

For more than two decades it was an invisible Germany about which most Americans knew as little as they did of Communist China. This was, in part, because neither West Germany nor the Western powers recognized its claim to exist as a separate country, and in part because the East German government was so suspicious of Western visitors that it allowed only a handful in to see what life and conditions were like.

What these visitors saw usually confirmed their suspicions or supported their preconceived notions.

This part of Germany has always been the poorer part. It was a region of inferior soil with light and scant industry, much of which had been carted off by the Russians after the war as reparations. Its regime seemed a mere fig leaf for continuing military government. In fact, compared with the West, conditions were so much worse that between 1945 and 1961 some 3.5 million East Germans fled to the Federal Republic.

In August 1961, to halt this mass exodus that was draining the lifeblood from the GDR, a wall was built around East Berlin and the country's borders were fortified with barbed wire, mine fields, watchtowers, sentry dogs, and armed guards under orders to shoot anyone leaving the country without permission.

East Germans, with few exceptions, were barred from leaving. The vast majority of West Germans were prohibited from visiting them. West Berliners were not allowed to see their friends and relatives in the eastern part of the city, even when they lived only a few blocks away or across the street. Letters from neighboring villages, divided by the

8

border, sometimes took longer to reach their destinations than mail from halfway around the world. Relatives who wanted to meet had to find neutral ground far from home— the beaches of Communist Bulgaria and Romania where tens of thousands of East and West Germans, listed officially as tourists, could hold family reunions.

To picture this in America you would have to imagine the city of Washington cut in half along Pennsylvania Avenue by a 12-foot-high wall. There would be barbed wire running from the Canadian border to the Gulf of Mexico, dividing the Dakotas from Minnesota, Nebraska from Iowa, Kansas from Missouri, Oklahoma from Arkansas, Texas from Louisiana. For a man from Kansas City, Missouri, to see his sister living in Kansas City, Kansas, both might have to go on vacation to Mexico.

It was not the first time in history that a powerful ruler had walled in his domain. But this wall, built by Walter Ulbricht, then the most powerful man in East Germany, was unique as the first in history designed to keep a nation's subjects in, rather than its enemies out.

Cruel and inhumane as this seemed to those personally affected, the wall accomplished what it was supposed to. It ended the flow of humanity that was bleeding East Germany of its labor force, its most important economic asset. The GDR began to consolidate. When people could no longer leave easily, they began to accept the East German state for better or worse. A form of East German patriotism, based on pride of achievement and on different values than those in West Germany, began to develop.

Today though still poorer and far less glittering than West Germany, the GDR has arrived. It has entered the exclusive circle of the world's top ten industrial nations. It is the most prosperous Communist country of all, second only to the Soviet Union itself in overall industrial capacity, but way ahead of the USSR in engineering skills, technological know-how and sophistication, and above all, in its standard of living.

The wall also sealed Germany's division. Two Germanys with different social, economic, and political systems—one patterned after America's, the other after Russia's—exist in the world today. They are products of the breakup of the wartime alliance between the United States and the Soviet Union and of the Cold War that poisoned relations between Washington and Moscow for more than two decades after the common defeat of Hitler's Germany.

The two nations have virtually the same flag—horizontal bars of black, red, and gold—the only difference being that East Germany's has a round seal of grain shoots, and a hammer and a compass. They speak the same language, though with widely varying dialects. Yet for almost twenty-five years they refused to recognize each other. They would not even acknowledge that the other existed. Although the two states continued to trade with each other to the tune of $6 million yearly, relations between them consisted of little more than mutual name-calling and the exchange of the loudest, vilest propaganda blasts the world had ever heard. Each seemed bent on painting the other in the darkest possible shades in a shouting match of insults.

That was the story of the two Germanys until Willy Brandt became chancellor—that is, prime minister—of the Federal Republic in October 1969. Brandt devised a new formula. Although there is only one German people, he said, there can be two German states. At some future date they might rejoin by peaceful means. Meanwhile there was no harm in recognizing their independence from each other.

In March 1970 Brandt traveled to the East German city

of Erfurt for a summit meeting with Willi Stoph, at that time the GDR's prime minister. That initial "Willy-Willi" conference, as the papers called it, was the first time representatives of the two countries had talked to each other officially. Soon after, Stoph came to the West German city of Kassel for a return match. By early 1971 a whole series of East-West German meetings was under way. Their aim was to find a means for the two states to coexist peacefully.

Finally in December 1972 a basic treaty between the two Germanys was signed. In it both countries promised not to use force against each other, to respect their social, economic, and political systems, and to exchange permanent diplomatic representatives who would be ambassadors in everything but name. The treaty, moreover, provided for a relaxation of travel restrictions and set up certain guarantees for the independence and security of West Berlin and for its links to West Germany.

In June 1973, after the treaty had been ratified by the West and East German parliaments, a symbolic ceremony took place in Bonn's Schaumburg Palace, the West German White House.

Facing each other to exchange signed, sealed, and leather-bound copies of the treaty, stood two middle-aged men: Michael Kohl, a senior official of the East German prime minister's office, and Egon Bahr, a member of the West German cabinet. For months they had done the tough, nit-picking negotiating that made the treaty possible. Both were Germans and spoke the same sing-song Thuringian dialect. In fact both had been born in the same German province—in villages less than fifty miles apart. Both had served in wartime *Wehrmacht* and for almost half of their lives—until May 8, 1945—had been citizens of the same German Reich. Yet the documents in their hands signified the first formal recognition of the two Germanys by each other. Foreigners who watched the exchange felt there was something slightly Alice-in-Wonderland about it all.

Soon after that ceremony dozens of other countries, including the United States, began extending diplomatic recognition to East Germany and a number of Communist countries established diplomatic ties with West Germany.

In the fall of 1973 both Germanys were admitted to membership in the United Nations as separate countries. Though division now seemed irreversible, relations between the two Germanys had suddenly entered a new era of peaceful coexistence that would have seemed impossible only a few years earlier.

What kind of Germanys are they? How does life in them compare? How did they really become divided, and what prospects, if any, exist for their reunification?

Those are the questions this book will try to answer.

1
The Wall: Germany's Bleeding Wound

December is Germany's foggiest month. From the Danish border in the north to the craggy Alps of southern Bavaria, from the Rhine in the west to the Oder in the east, billows of fog—fluffy, white, and opaque—settle on the fields and in the valleys every evening as soon as the last shimmers of the pale winter sun have turned into the slate gray of dusk. Like huge wads of cotton, they hide human movements only a few feet away and muffle every sound.

These are the nights when the Germans of days past spun their folk legends and fairy tales; when the shrieks of the owls in the forest turned into choked cries; when children scurried closer to the hearth fires and huddled around their mothers'. skirts, convinced that goblins and witches, wolves, and robber barons were rampaging outside.

13

It was on this kind of December night in 1971 that Lothar Jahn, a twenty-one-year-old East German, watched the first tufts of fog roll into the little dale just south of the West German town of Duderstadt. From his carefully chosen hiding place, within a stone's throw of the first barbed wire fence that marks the border, he could see lights flicker on one by one in farmhouses and hear an occasional car or truck on the highway in West Germany.

"Soon," Lothar whispered, turning to his beautiful ash-blond wife, Jutta, squatting and shivering next to him. Jutta nodded and drew a blanket more snugly around Heike, their eleven-month-old baby girl, sleeping soundly in her arms.

Lothar waited—until the fog snuffed out the last of the flickering West German lights, until it smothered into silence the sounds of the West German automobiles, until it was so thick he could no longer see the East German barbed-wire fence.

"Now," he hissed, nudging Jutta slightly. The two groped through the fog toward the first fortification, strands of which Lothar cut with pliers to make a hole large enough to crawl through. They began picking their way gingerly across the plowed strip of land mines between the first and second barbed wire fences.

Lothar was just a step or two from Jutta when a deafening thud rent the air. It tossed the young woman a few feet up, then sent her crashing and screaming back to the ground, her baby still clutched in her arms. The mine had mangled both her legs.

Lothar, his face lacerated but otherwise not seriously injured, shouted crazily for help and tried to comfort his wife who writhed in pain on the ground. The baby, unharmed but awakened by the shock, screamed desperately.

Fortunately for the Jahns, the explosion and their cries

were not heard by East German border guards, who would have captured them and perhaps even left Jutta to bleed to death, but by a Duderstadt farmer living nearby. He alerted West German customs police who, risking their own lives, cut through the other fence and pulled the couple to safety over the minefield. They were rushed to the hospital where surgeons amputated Jutta's legs, one above, the other below the knee.

Maimed, scarred, and crippled—physically and mentally —Lothar and Jutta Jahn and their daughter Heike now live in West Germany.

Their story is tragic, but it is hardly unique. Dramatic, successful escapes from East to West as well as unsuccessful attempts that end in tragedy make headlines like these in West German newspapers almost every day:

THREE SWIM ACROSS ELBE RIVER TO FREEDOM

NINE EAST GERMANS DIG TUNNEL TO WEST BERLIN

TWO EAST GERMANS HALTED AT BORDER; THREE SUCCEED

SHOTS AT BORDER: ESCAPE BELIEVED HALTED

ATTEMPT TO FLEE ENDS IN BORDER BLOODBATH.

The border that divides the two Germanys was relatively easy to pass from 1945, when it was drawn as a demarcation line between the Soviet and Western occupation zones, until August 1961. Until 1952 police patrols were posted sparsely and watchtowers, where they existed at all, were few and far apart. You could go from one part of Germany to the other merely by walking across the fields and through the forests and the worst that could happen would be to get caught by a border patrol and be turned back. Moreover East Germans were permitted to travel legally to the West on vacations. If they wanted to defect they simply did not return home. As more and more fled across the borders, the

East German authorities clamped down. In 1952 travel restrictions were imposed and the borders tightened up. In 1956 they became even tighter.

But there was always Berlin, virtually an open city in which a five-cent subway ticket or a stroll from one side of the street to the other was all it took to travel between communism and capitalism. And from West Berlin you could simply take a plane to West Germany.

Thus in the first sixteen years after World War II, some 3.5 million East Germans came to the West. Some were victims of political persecution or felt they could not live in the dictatorial atmosphere of the GDR. Many more merely wanted to be reunited with relatives who had always lived in the West or had fled there on an earlier occasion. But the vast majority came for purely economic reasons. Life in West Germany was better than in the East.

"You can get ahead here if you want to," said one young refugee who fled in 1960. "And everything looks brighter. I was in West Berlin once before, eight years ago, and the lights and displays in the shop windows were something I just couldn't forget."

More than one-fourth of those who left the East before 1961 were young people between eighteen and twenty-five years of age, looking for more opportunity in life than they thought East Germany's communist system offered them.

In those years of the Cold War, Western propaganda pointed to the two Germanys as the great rivals in the contest between communism and capitalism. East Germany's lower standard of living and the mass exodus of its people were offered as proof by the West that communism was bad and could not work.

No doubt there is plenty wrong with communism and as an economic system it has proven very inefficient and pro-

duces a low standard of living. But as far as the contest between the two Germanys goes, it was lopsided from the start
and Communist Germany could not have won it, no matter
how hard it tried.

Germany's west was rich in anthracite, iron ore, and other
minerals; the east was poor, except for large deposits of
lignite and potash. The west had been the hub of the old
Reich's heavy industry, the east merely its finishing shop.
While West Germany was being pump-primed after the end
of World War II with CARE packets, gifts, grants, and
nearly $4 billion in Marshall Plan aid from America, East
Germany was being squeezed like a lemon by the Russians.
With less than one-third of the population it was paying the
war debts of Germany as a whole—about $23 million, ac-
cording to Western estimates.

To complicate matters, the men who ruled East Germany
were trying to force an unpopular system down the throats
of the people. Private farming was all but abolished and replaced by forced collectivization. Factories were taken from
their owners and operated by the government. The few
flickers of democracy that had survived the twelve years of
Hitler's dictatorship were snuffed out.

It is no wonder that the eastern part of Germany could
not keep pace with the west and that it ranked high among
territories likely to be depopulated.

The tragedy of this mass migration, gleefully encouraged
by West Germany and the Western allies who milked it
for its propaganda value, was that the more people who left,
the worse matters got.

The chaos caused by this sixteen-year-long exodus defies
description. Day after day in any village or city, a factory
hand would be gone, a miner would fail to show up for his
shift, a farmer would disappear from the fields. Shops would

remain shut because their owners had defected. School children would come to class only to find their teacher missing, and patients waited in vain for doctors who had deserted them for more lucrative practices in the West.

Conditions were so desperate that factory managers did not know from one day to the next how many workers they would have or which machines would be attended, which ones not. With no reserves to draw on, the flight of one mechanic, machinist, construction worker, technician, or engineer touched off a chain reaction that brought East Germany closer to collapse every day.

"The entire economy is falling apart," one refugee from a small East German town told me in 1960. "One day four bus drivers left and the buses were off schedule. People were late for work, which slowed down production. There was no one in the shops to serve you, which probably didn't really matter as most shops had almost nothing left to sell."

To plug one hole in the dike the government made new ones. It tried everything, but being dictatorial and communist, it used mostly threats and pressure to stem the tide. The greater the threats and the tighter the restrictions which it imposed, the greater the exodus became and with it the chaos.

Worst of all, the refugees were the cream of the GDR's labor force: the best educated, the youngest, the most capable, the most needed, for these were the ones who knew they stood the greatest chance of making good in West Germany.

Of course the movement was not entirely a one-way street. Between 1950 and 1961 an estimated half-million people went from West Germany to the GDR. Some were Communists or left-wing idealists who went for political reasons. Many went east because of family ties. One-third to one-half were East Germans who had fled to the West but were returning because they had been disappointed, had failed to make good, or were simply homesick. Among them were many teenagers who had done their running away from home by fleeing west and were now returning to their parents.

But this reverse refugee movement could not make up for the westward flow, and by the summer of 1961 East Germany had lost about 20 per cent of its postwar population. Thousands more were fleeing every week. The regime felt it had no choice but to shut the gates.

At 1:11 A.M. Sunday, August 13, 1961, East Berliners were jolted out of their sleep by the clatter of tanks, the rat-tat-tat of motorcycles, and the deep rumble of truck engines in the dark and empty cobblestone streets. Those who peeked from behind their curtains saw convoys of grim-faced People's Policemen, or *Vopos,* and steel-helmeted troops of the National People's Army moving toward the 28-mile-long frontier that divides East from West Berlin.

At 80 crossover points and intersections the trucks and armored cars disgorged troops, bales of barbed wire, concrete and steel posts, picks, shovels, and jackhammers. Through the night soldiers and policemen built barricades, rolled out wire entanglements, erected fences, and dug up streets and sidewalks to improvise trenches and car traps.

Other squads rushed to lock up elevated and subway stations that led to trains servicing West Berlin. Telephone connections between the two halves of the city were cut. Within East Germany itself rail traffic ground to a halt and thousands of travelers were taken off trains for Berlin and ordered back to their homes.

Machine-gun-, rifle-and-bayonet-brandishing soldiers and police, backed by armored trucks with high-pressure water cannons, stood a grim watch over the barriers that sealed off East from West Berlin.

All along the border between the two Germanys, from the Baltic Sea in the north to the city of Hof in the south, new barbed wire was strung, old fences repaired. New tank traps, watchtowers, and road barriers were put up and new mines laid in the death strip that parallels the demarcation line.

By Tuesday, August 15, police and army engineers began replacing the barbed-wire obstacles in East Berlin with slabs of concrete to form the Berlin Wall.

Only three official crossover points remained in the divided city itself, and four highways, seven rail lines, one canal, and three air corridors cut across the border—primarily for traffic between West Germany and isolated West Berlin. More than 30 other railway lines and 111 roads and highways which had once interconnected the eastern and western parts of Germany ended dead at the border—avenues leading to nowhere.

These were days of desperate, daredevil escapes and human tragedy.

A mason helping to build the wall near the Brandenburg Gate waited until a truck blocked the vision of the nearest *Vopo* guard, then climbed over the wall himself.

Submachine gun on his back, his helmet strapped tightly under his chin, an East German army sergeant broke away from a group of border guards and took a flying leap over a roll of barbed wire into the West.

On Bernauer Strasse, where the street and sidewalks are West Berlin territory, but the apartment houses on one side belong to the East, dozens of tenants jumped to the nets spread by West Berlin firemen or climbed down gingerly

An East German soldier escapes to a new life in the West.

c.1

from their bedroom windows along ropes fashioned from sheets and bath towels.

In a West Berlin hospital a woman had died of cancer and had been taken to a cemetery just east of the sector border the day before it was sealed off. Her husband, arriving too late, had to stare silently over the cemetery wall as other relatives buried her.

One West Berlin couple was married right next to the wall so the bride's mother could watch the ceremony from the other side.

The rest of the world looked on with stunned disbelief. There were protests, petitions, and silent marches to express Western indignation. There were displays of force between Soviet and American tanks at Checkpoint Charlie, one of the few remaining crossover points between East and West Berlin.

But the wall stayed and twelve years later, as this is being written, it is still there, ugly as ever and still a symbol of man's inhumanity to man. And yet for East Germany's rulers it accomplished what they intended. It reduced the flood of refugees to a trickle, put the GDR's economy on its feet, and changed the course of history.

Some 3.5 million had fled before the wall was built and the border sealed. In the first decade after that, there were only 34,455, including some 3,000 border guards. No one knows how many more tried but failed. The grimmest figure is of those who died in the attempt: 92 at the border and another 65 at the Berlin wall itself during the ten years after August 13, 1961. They were either shot by East German border guards or killed by land mines.

They continue to flee and they are still being killed.

Every third day West German frontier police record shots

fired or mines detonated on the other side, though some of the mines are set off by forest animals and some of the shots are fired at deer and rabbits that the guards mistake for refugees.

On the average some 400 East Germans make it to West Germany every month, though only a fourth of them escape across the border or the wall directly. The majority go west by less dangerous means. They jump East German ships in neutral harbors or off friendly foreign shores. They take advantage of the more relaxed rules in some other Communist countries and escape from there during vacations.

Many are smuggled out of East Germany with fake passports and travel documents, in the false-bottomed trunks of automobiles, or the trick gas tanks of big overland trucks by a Europe-wide network of professional escape agencies.

Some of these agencies are sponsored by international religious organizations and are motivated by purely selfless considerations. Many more, however, are strictly commercial and profit-minded, charging as much as $20,000 per refugee. They have taken to offering their services in thinly disguised advertisements in Swiss, German, and Austrian newspapers. All too often they collect their money from unsuspecting relatives in advance, then either bungle the escape job or double-cross the refugee by reporting him to the East German secret police.

The wall is a symbol of man's inhumanity to man as well as of his hunger for profit, even at the expense of another's suffering. However, it is also a tribute to his inventiveness.

The East Germans who have fled since August 1961 have used just about everything but helicopters and rockets. Escapees have tunneled under the border, swum around it, flown over it, tightroped across it, and rammed through it

23

with armor-plated trucks and buses. The gentlemanly way, however, is to simply outwit the border guards with fake documents and a straight face.

One of the cleverest underground railways was thought up by a West Berliner who spirited 180 East Germans, disguised as foreign diplomats, to the west. He used long black shiny limousines from a car-rental agency and leather-covered, official-looking documents originally printed as membership cards in a fancy West German playboy club called Confédération Diplomatique. The initials CD, gold-embossed on the cards, seemed to stand for diplomatic corps and made them look like diplomatic passports. At that time, in the mid-1960s, East Germany was so eager to win diplomatic recognition from non-Communist countries that border guards would not have dared to ask questions of anyone who looked like a foreign diplomat.

An even bolder escape was staged by four East Germans who passed through Checkpoint Charlie disguised as Soviet Army officers. They wore homemade Russian uniforms and drove out in a Soviet-made car which they had painted regulation olive green. The East German guards actually saluted them.

One East Berliner even managed to escape across the border backwards. A professional photographer, he hired several good-looking girls as models and took them to Checkpoint Charlie where he told the border guards he was on assignment for an East German magazine to take publicity pictures of the frontier arrangements. He asked several of the guards to pose with the girls. His back to the West Berlin side of the border, he began taking photos, and with each picture he took one or two steps backward— closer to West Berlin. One of the guards posing for him called out, half laughing, "Hey, comrade, watch out. If you go too far back you'll end up in West Berlin and the Americans will grab you." The photographer told him not to worry and kept shooting pictures—until he was close enough to the white demarcation line to step across it, then turn and run.

It is a strange sort of border. From the Baltic Sea in the north to the little hamlet of Prex in the south where East and West Germany meet Czechoslovakia, it zigs and zags, climbs and falls through lakes and ponds, woods and fields, farms and villages, houses and barnyards, rivers and creeks.

It bristles with barbed wire, mesh fences, watchtowers, searchlights, plowed strips of no man's land, two million mines, and a network of shrapnel-shooting automatic booby traps. It measures 835.8 miles in length (plus the 28 miles dividing Berlin), and each year the GDR spends an estimated $350 million to maintain it and to pay the 60,000 soldiers of the National People's Army who stand guard over it. Facing them, from the West German side, stand 20,000 members of the FRG's frontier police and two divisions of Allied troops, including some 6,000 Americans.

Both sides have milked the wall for maximum propaganda mileage. West Berlin maintains a Wall Museum and tourists, especially important foreign dignitaries, after passing through the museum are taken to a platform, handed binoculars, and encouraged to stare at the East German guards on the other side. The East Germans, also equipped with field glasses, stare back. When important visitors arrive in East Berlin, one of the sight-seeing high points on their schedules is a trip to the East German Wall Museum near the Brandenburg Gate. It too has a raised platform nearby from which they can look at the "capitalist menace" on the West Berlin side.

The most macabre thing about the wall is a game named

Here in Berlin, the wall is a dramatic symbol of the divided Germanys.

for it that children on both sides play. "Wall" is just like cops and robbers or cowboys and Indians with plenty of shooting, fake death, and violence. The only difference is that the participants are called "refugees" and "guards."

The border cuts villages in half—like Mödlareuth, near the city of Hof, where as long as people could remember the village school had stood in Thuringia, now East Germany, and the local church in Bavaria, now part of West Germany.

Until 1952 Mödlareuth remained pretty much one hamlet, despite the border. Children living on the western side went to school in the east. On Sundays parishioners from the east came to church on the western side of town. Then a wooden picket fence was put up and people were no longer allowed to go back and forth. In 1956 the fence was replaced by barbed wire and a mine field. Eventually a concrete wall like the one in Berlin was built.

The frontier bisects farmers' fields and in some places even cuts right through farmhouses. That is the case in Phillipsthal, a little West German town in Hesse, where one farmhouse straddles the line. For a number of years its owner and his family slept in their East German bedrooms but ate meals and relaxed in their West German dining and living rooms. One night in 1961, afraid that the East Germans might eventually make him subject to their laws, the farmer moved all his belongings to the western side of the house and walled up the doors to the east. He was left with only half a house, but that, he said, was better than being "all communist."

It is also a border ideal for spying and mysteries.

Take the strange case of the field hand who showed up looking for a job in 1961 in Mechow, a village on the western side. He hired on with a prosperous local farmer whose fertile grain and grazing land was right next to the frontier. The man was a good, hard worker, but he was a bit odd. A bachelor with no known friends or relatives, he was a loner and very secretive. One day in 1971 he was killed when the tractor he was driving ran off the road. Local police and county officials did not know whom to contact with word of his death. In the hope of finding some clue, they broke into the dead man's locked room. There they discovered a high-powered Soviet radio transmitter with which the "field hand" apparently had been sending espionage information to the east for ten years.

The border of course is also a reflection of the changing relationship between the two Germanys, their attitudes toward each other, and their place in the world.

For two years after the wall was built virtually the only contact between the two countries were radio and TV programs which could be seen by many on both sides of the frontier. The first break came in 1963 when the GDR decided to permit West Berliners to visit their close relatives in the eastern part of the city for Christmas holidays. Those happy reunions took place three times yearly for the next few years until the spring of 1967 when the GDR government shut the gates as suddenly as it had opened them.

For the following five years the only legal westward movement was by East German pensioners who were allowed to visit relatives once a year for up to 30 days. Since these elderly citizens were a drain on the GDR's treasury, East German officials hoped they would not return. But the vast majority did; for many, pensions in the GDR have a higher purchasing power than in the FRG.

Virtually the only West Germans allowed into the GDR were businessmen and visitors to the semiannual trade fairs in the city of Leipzig.

The next crack in the wall came in 1972. East Germany's aim in sealing its borders had been twofold. In addition to wanting to stop the refugee flow, it wanted to enforce the reality of two Germanys and to dramatize the claim to separate sovereignty that West Germany and the Western Allies had refused to acknowledge. But when Willy Brandt became chancellor of the Federal Republic, he decided that the more realistic policy of recognizing East Germany might lead to better relations and a better deal for people in both Germanys. As a result of his policy the wall began to lose some of its purpose and things started to loosen up again.

In 1972 West Berliners were again allowed to visit relatives in East Berlin—and not just on important holidays. Traffic to and from West Berlin became less restricted than at any time since the end of the war. For the first time in almost twenty years, West Germans and West Berliners were allowed to travel to East Germany and East Berlin as ordinary tourists.

In June 1973 when the basic treaty between the two Germanys became law, holes were knocked into the border itself. Fifteen more highways and seven more rail lines were opened up to handle the expected increase in traffic. Most important of all some 6.5 million West Germans and an estimated 2 million East Germans who live close to the border are now entitled, on paper at least, to travel back and forth for one-day trips as many as thirty times a year. In practice, there is little two-way traffic as very few East Germans have gotten permission to leave. But at least West German relatives were allowed to visit them again, and within the first few weeks after the new rule was in force, thousands of West Germans took advantage of it.

For the first time since 1952 residents of western Mödlareuth could see their kin and friends in the eastern part of town. The only hitch: They would have to take a bus many miles out of their way, for Mödlareuth's main street is not a crossover point itself.

Over the years the East–West German border has been called all sorts of names. To East German propagandists it has been the "anti-imperialist," the "peace," and the "realistic" frontier. To West Germans it has been the "border of death," a "bloody border," and the "frontier of shame."

A young West German farmer who tills his fields within sight of it once called it simply, "an arbitrary border."

It is that and it is not.

It is arbitrary because of the way it was drawn up, without much thought, by the Allied powers toward the close of World War II. On the other hand there is a certain logic to the arbitrariness. At the time when it was drawn, Germany, as a united nation, had existed only seventy-five years. For most of its history before then it had been even more divided than it is today.

2
Germany or Germanys?

What is Germany and who are the Germans? Simple as that question sounds, answering it is easier said than done.

It cannot accurately be described as a country in Europe with clearly defined borders such as those which have marked France, Spain, and Portugal for many centuries. That description applies to less than eighty years of history. Those eight decades began in 1871 when Prince Otto von Bismarck, the prime minister of Prussia, created a German nation-state out of a jigsaw map of little kingdoms, principalities, and duchies, each of which jealously guarded its rights and privileges. The period ended in 1949 when the West German Federal Republic and the East German Democratic Republic were formally established as separate countries.

31

In fact until 1871 Germany was often and correctly called "the Germanys" even by Bismarck himself.

Even defining the German language raises some problems, for there are two languages and numerous dialects.

The official and most widely used language is High German. It is part of a language category that includes Pennsylvania Dutch and Yiddish, and is spoken in its best and purest form in what used to be the old Kingdom of Hanover. Its dialects are so varied and numerous that to the untrained ear a tourist busload of High German speakers conversing in their native Bavarian, Swabian, Hessian, Rhinelandish, Westphalian, Berliner, Saxonian, and Thuringian dialects would sound like a Tower of Babel on wheels.

The other language—and it is a language not a dialect—spoken in the northwestern part of Germany, is Low German. It is closely related to Dutch, Flemish, Afrikaans, and nearer to English than it is to High German.

Even the word "German" is not German but Latin; it means "one who is of the same blood." The Romans called the barbarian people who inhabited a good part of what is now Germany the "Germani." The Germans themselves call their country "Deutschland" and the language and the people "Deutsch." The word is believed to have come from an ancient High German word, "diot," meaning, "the people." The English, who speak a derivative of Low German, never could pronounce the word "Deutsch" properly and got around it by saying "Dutch," by which they really did not mean the people and language of Holland but Germany. When Germans showed up in Colonial Pennsylvania in the eighteenth century, the English colonists already there called them the "Pennsylvania Dutch," which is what they are called today, although they never had anything to do with Holland.

The Germanic peoples are a great ethnic complex who today inhabit most of Western Europe: Sweden, Norway,
Denmark, Iceland, Germany, Austria, Switzerland, northern
Italy, the Netherlands, Belgium, Luxembourg, northern and
central France, lowland Scotland, and England. In a way
most West Europeans are of Germanic origin.

On the other hand the Prussians, long regarded—incor-
rectly—as the most Germanic of all Germans because of
their reputation for discipline, military skill, orderliness, and
industriousness, were not of German but of Slavic and Baltic
origin. They had been conquered and subjugated by Germans in the thirteenth century.

Defining Germany and the Germans thus is no easy task,
and the attempt has given more than one scholar sleepless
nights.

The first-known sign of human life in what is now considered Germany was an ape-like creature who lived 500,000
years ago. His fossil jaw was found in 1907 near Heidelberg,
which is why he is called Heidelberg Man. The next sign of
a human type was Neanderthal Man, who inhabited the
Neander Valley near Düsseldorf 60,000 years ago.

It is difficult to say just when the primitive tribes, later
called the Germani, first emerged from Asia into Central
Europe, driving the Celts, a group of people who had been
living in southwestern Germany and eastern France since
about 2,000 B.C., further westward and eventually across the
English Channel to Scotland, Ireland, and Wales. Most his-
torians believe that the process of Germanic intrusion into
Central Europe must have begun about 1,000 B.C. and that
it lasted for about ten centuries. These Germanic peoples
were first mentioned by a fourth century B.C. Greek naviga-
tor who sailed as far north as Norway and Jutland. Their
real entry into recorded history, however, was not until the

first century B.C. when the Romans tried but failed to conquer them.

Julius Caesar, no pacifist himself, described them as fiercely warlike. On the other hand, Tacitus, a Roman historian who devoted an entire book to them, glorified their simple way of life as contrasted with the immorality and corruption of his native Rome.

The first showdown between Romans and Germans was in the year 9 A.D. Three Roman legions were defeated by a Germanic tribe, the Cheruschi, led by their chieftain Hermann (Arminius) in the battle of the Teutoburg Forest, about forty miles southwest of what is now the city of Hanover. The site of the battle is a national shrine today and Hermann a German hero.

The Teutoburg Forest was the northeasternmost point the Romans reached. Although they continued to clash with the Germans and even avenged their defeat by the Cheruschi, they made no other real attempt to penetrate deeply into Germany.

Instead the Romans colonized the areas south of the Danube and west of the Rhine, establishing large cities and military camps such as Cologne, Bonn, Trier, Augsburg, Regensburg, and Vienna. To protect the territory they controlled, they built the Limes, a defensive wall some three hundred miles long, which zigzagged from near Cologne on the Rhine to Regensburg on the Danube.

The Limes was Germany's first division. The Germanic people living west and south of it soon adopted many Roman customs and modes of thought which distinguish them from the Germans living further east and north to this day.

In the fourth century A.D., as the western Roman empire neared collapse, the German tribes east of the Limes began expanding south and west. The Goths, an East Germanic people and the first to have a written language, and the Vandals drove into Italy. The Burgundii descended on the territory that still bears their name. The Alemannii settled in eastern France. The tribes from the Elbe and Denmark, such as the Jutes, the Angles and some of the Saxons, crossed the sea to England.

There were many others: the Lombards, the Visigoths, the Franks, the Teutons, the Suebi (Swabians), the Boiarii (Bavarians), the Avars, the Marcomannii. They had fought Celts, the Romans, and each other. They intermarried with the peoples they conquered just as they intermarried with those that conquered them. As they moved west and south the Slavs drove in, settling the territories the Germanic tribes had left behind.

This migration of peoples lasted several centuries, and by the time it came to a halt in the early seventh century A.D., the face of Europe had been transformed. The old Roman Empire was dead, with power vested in the eastern emperor at Byzantium. The various Germanic peoples, melded with what had remained of the Celts and Romans, dominated central and western Europe. The Franks, Burgundii, and Alemannii became the French of more recent times. In fact the French word for Germany is *Allemagne* and the German word for France is *Frankreich,* literally, "empire of the Franks." The Lombards and the Venetians stayed in Italy to mix with the Romans and become Italians. The Goths and Visigoths became the Spaniards. The Angles and those Saxons who had left the mainland became Englishmen. The Helvetii became the Swiss.

East of the Rhine, between the old Roman Limes and the advancing Slavs, lived those tribes which became the Germans of later times. These were the Saxons, or at least that

35

major part of them which had not gone to England, the Swabians, the Frisians, and the Bavarians (who may have been more Celtic than Germanic). Similarities of language began to develop—the beginnings of High German in the south and east, Low German in the northwest.

West of the Rhine a new empire, that of the Franks, began to take shape under a powerful king—Charles the Great, or Charlemagne. For more than forty years, from 771 to 814, he fought many wars, most of them against the pagan Saxons. With forced conversions to Christianity, massacres, and the deportation of thousands of Saxons to the interior of his Frankish kingdom, he established control over Saxony, finally defeating the Saxons' most powerful leader, the chieftain Widukuind, in 785. It is hard to say which blood ran thicker in Charles' veins—that of the future Frenchmen or that of the old Germans. Today both French and Germans claim him as a great hero. His empire stretched from the English Channel and the Atlantic Ocean to the Elbe River, from the Mediterranean and the Po River to the North Sea.

On Christmas Day in the year 800 A.D. Pope Leo III crowned Charles emperor in Rome. The title—in German it was *Kaiser,* that is, Caesar—implied that Charlemagne was the Christian successor to the Roman caesars and with that act the Holy Roman Empire was born.

Charlemagne was a remarkable man for his time. He was a brilliant soldier and an able administrator, and he encouraged learning. He had vision. He wanted to restore order to the chaos and bring light to the Dark Ages that the Germanic tribes had brought to Europe. But his new empire was based on the false notion that old Rome had merely been suspended. He forgot about the eastern emperors who continued to rule from Byzantium until the thirteenth century and claimed to be the legal heirs. Moreover Germanic Europe was too divided and too primitive to re-create the glory that had been Rome's.

In name Charlemagne's Holy Roman Empire lasted for a thousand years, until 1806 when Francis II of Austria renounced the title under pressure from a new emperor—Napoleon. But for most of its lifespan the empire was largely fiction.

In fact it barely survived Charlemagne's own reign, for in 843 the West Franks seceded from the original empire to form the nucleus of what was to become France, with a language based on Latin rather than German. The realm of the East Franks went to one of Charlemagne's grandsons, Louis the German. Charlemagne's eldest grandson, Lothair, kept the title of Holy Roman Emperor. But he got only a narrow strip of land, running from Belgium through Burgundy into Italy—the "Middle Kingdom"—over which the East and West Franks, later known as Germans and French, were to fight for centuries.

For the next century or so there were a number of emperors, each weaker than his predecessor, numerous pretenders, and continuing warfare among the chieftains, dukes, and kings who ruled the Germanic lands. The imperial idea itself eroded and was not revived until a powerful Saxon king, Otto I, came to rule over the Middle Kingdom. Otto was crowned emperor in Rome in 962, the first real German to have the title. It remained with the Germans and Austrians from then on. In theory it was an elective office; in practice the title became hereditary starting in 1438 when the imperial crown went to the Hapsburg family with whom it remained until the end.

Although the territorial boundaries of the Holy Roman Empire varied, they usually included present-day Germany,

Austria, Bohemia, Moravia, sections of Northern Italy, Belgium, and until 1648, Holland and Switzerland. The emperors claimed to be the supreme rulers of all Christendom, but their authority, even within Germany and Austria, was limited. In France, Southern Italy, Denmark, Sweden, Poland, Hungary, England, and Spain it was nonexistent.

As Voltaire, the eighteenth-century French philosopher, once said, "This agglomeration which was called and which still calls itself the Holy Roman Empire is neither holy, nor Roman, nor an empire."

The empire—the German word is *Reich*—was an illusion with grave, long-term consequences for German history. In one sense the Germans are still paying for the imperial idea today. Hitler's war had the mad aim of revitalizing it. Even the name which Hitler chose—The Thousand-Year Reich— was a reference to the thousand years of the Holy Roman Empire.

On the one hand the empire was a substitute for the unified monarchy the Germanys lacked. On the other hand its existence became a major obstacle to the creation of such a centralized monarchy, and to German unity as such.

Of course it might be argued that these Holy Roman emperors were really nothing more than kings of Austro-Germany who enjoyed playing Roman Caesar in a post-Roman age. If they insisted on calling themselves kaisers it was their business. That would be a valid argument if they had had the same power as the kings of England and France, Sweden and Spain. But the real power rested with tribal chieftains who later became the barons, counts, dukes, electors, prince-bishops, and kings of the various German states. By the middle of the seventeenth century there were some 350 of these.

There were other reasons, of course, why a unified monarchy did not take hold in medieval Germany as it had in medieval France and England.

For many centuries the emperors had no permanent capital and wandered from palace to palace. Later the wandering stopped, but the capital still moved, being the palace of whichever king or duke had been named emperor. It was really not until the imperial crown went permanently to the Hapsburg dynasty that a true capital, Vienna, developed.

Since the power of the emperors rested largely on the size and wealth of their own hereditary kingdoms or duchies, they naturally tended to concern themselves more with their own lands than with the affairs of the empire.

Moreover the empire had no fixed geographical boundaries, especially to the east and south.

Lacking real power, the emperors were unable to control and establish their authority over the barons, counts, dukes, and princes who warred ruthlessly among each other and whose numbers grew as their lands were subdivided by their children. Just as Charlemagne's realm had once been split into three kingdoms among his grandsons, so the fiefs and duchies were divided. One result of this, besides continuous subdivision, was that the emperors encouraged the establishment of "free imperial cities," which owed their loyalty to no baron or count, only to the emperor himself. To protect themselves from feuding tribes, robber barons, and brigands, these cities built massive defensive walls and tended to become increasingly self-reliant. Thus began the great German tradition of trade and craftsmanship. But it also fostered provincialism.

There was also the uniquely German institution of prince-bishops and prince-abbots—church leaders who enjoyed earthly powers. Over the centuries they became immensely wealthy and independent rulers. Some of the richest and largest of these independent church states, such as Salzburg, were bigger and more influential than some of the dukedoms.

Culturally, artistically, and commercially the Germanys flourished in these centuries. Politically, however, they became more and more divided. In their foreign relations they became increasingly expansionistic, looking toward disunited Italy and at the primitive peoples to their east as sources of wealth and territory.

The Germans played a major role in the thirteenth century Crusades, during which the unique Order of the Teutonic Knights was born. Financed largely by the big trading cities of northern Germany such as Bremen and Lübeck, formally dedicated to relieving suffering and sickness, the order developed into a sort of military club with enormous political powers on the frontiers of Christendom.

In 1309 the order established its headquarters in Marienburg in what is now Soviet Latvia. The knights, besides being a formidable military force, were extremely rich and very smart businessmen who used the powers of the sword and their treasury to colonize Slavic Pomerania, Prussia, and the Baltic states in the name of Holy Roman Christianity.

Their power in this region lasted little more than a hundred years but left a permanent Germanic influence as well as a Slavic fear and hatred of things German that endures to the present day. When the order declined in the fifteenth century, its lands and riches passed into the hands of the Hohenzollern family from southern Germany. The Hohenzollerns eventually became the counts and dukes of Brandenburg, with their capital in Berlin, and then the kings of Prussia, and finally, in 1871, the kaisers of the Second Reich. Unfortunately the Hohenzollerns also employed many of the Teutonic Knights' military-economic techniques and policies of eastward expansion.

Curiously, however, over the centuries it has been neither German expansionism nor German trading skill which has really changed the world but German thought and ideas. Two Germans, both intellectuals and rebels, born 350 years apart, changed the world beyond recognition: Martin Luther and Karl Marx.

Luther appeared on the stage of history October 31, 1517, when he nailed his 95 theses, attacking the Roman clergy and its abuses, to the door of his church in Wittenberg. That was the beginning of the Protestant Reformation.

Protestantism, of course, is what Luther is known for best and it certainly changed world history. But Luther was responsible for other things as well, notably his translation of the Bible into German, which provided the basis for modern High German and extended the promise of literacy to the masses.

Lutheranism, however, also touched off a century of killing that culminated in the Thirty Years' War from 1618 to 1648. Ostensibly a war between Catholics and Protestants, it involved every German state, plus the Swedes, and turned into a power struggle between them. It was the longest and most fearsome civil war that Europe has ever experienced and when it finally ended with the Treaty of Westphalia, the Germanys were ravished lands. Nearly every city and town had been sacked and burned at least once and it has been estimated that nearly seven million people, about one third the total population of the German states, had been killed.

The war also reshaped the map of Germany and gave birth to new states. Switzerland and the Netherlands, both of which emerged Protestant from the struggle, received their independence from what had been the Holy Roman Empire. Vienna, staunchly Catholic, remained the empire's center of power. Its influence, however, barely extended north of the Main River line where two Protestant duchies —Saxony and Brandenburg-Prussia—began to flex their muscles.

In 1697 the ruler of Saxony was named King of Poland as well. To keep up with his rival, Frederick I of Prussia proclaimed his own duchy a kingdom in 1701. Frederick's son began amassing a large and well-trained army. His grandson, Frederick the Great, turned Prussia into a major European power. Under his rule Prussia fought and won two long wars with Austria, from which it gained large amounts of new territory. Then in 1795 Prussia tangled with revolutionary France and lost.

For the next twenty years German history was dominated largely by events in France and by Napoleon who, strange as it may seem, did more to influence the history of Germany than that of France.

Napoleon annexed the Rhineland and abolished more than a hundred of the smaller German states and the free cities, which were absorbed by the larger duchies. He also dissolved the bishopric-principalities, and secularized the monasteries, giving their lands and territories to those German duchies and kingdoms that promised to side with him. Most of them did, with the exception of Austria and Prussia.

Napoleon also abolished the by then meaningless Holy Roman Empire, compelling its last emperor, the defeated Francis of Austria, to renounce the title and position in 1806.

Most important, perhaps, that same year he rewarded his most dependable and loyal German satellites by converting them from grand duchies into kingdoms. These were Bavaria, Württemberg, and Saxony.

By 1813, however, following his defeat in Russia, Napoleon's German allies turned on him. Saxony and Württemberg joined in the drive against him that ended with his defeat at Waterloo in 1815.

The Germanys that emerged from the Napoleonic Wars were a vastly different breed of states than those with which the nineteenth century had opened. The wars had enlarged the territories of both Prussia and Austria, which now called itself an empire. The number of independent German states had been reduced to thirty-nine. Under the influence of Prince Clemens von Metternich, chancellor of Austria, a loose confederation of German states was formed. Its three most powerful members were Austria, which presided over the confederation, Prussia, and Bavaria.

For the next fifty-five years the Germanys presented a confusing picture. Local and regional loyalties were giving way to a new spirit of German national patriotism. At the same time, however, the thirty-nine members of the confederation tried to preserve every shred of their local privileges and sovereignty. Industry was expanding and with it trade, travel, and communications. But each of the thirty-nine states had its own currency, tax laws, customs regulations, postal system, foreign ministry, and army. As an example, when the first railroad was built from Berlin to Hamburg, a distance of about 150 miles, it required the approval of five separate governments. On paper the confederation was dedicated to the idea of German unity. But its two biggest members, Austria and Prussia, seemed continuously at each others' throats.

Although this period was relatively peaceful in the Ger-

43

manys and the rest of Europe, it was marked by rapid social change as a result of the industrial revolution. New ideas were being discussed—ideas of national independence in such countries as Hungary, ideas of national unity in Italy and Germany, ideas of economic and social change in France.

The most radical thinker of those days was a young German-born lawyer and social philosopher named Karl Marx who in 1842, at age twenty-four, became editor of a left-wing newspaper called the *Rheinische Zeitung.* No German since Martin Luther three hundred years before him was to change Germany, and the world, as much as Marx. The essence of his philosophy was that "inevitable laws" of history rather than the natural rights of man justified social reform. These laws, Marx said, would lead to the eventual triumph of the working class over capitalism. It is Marx's philosophy that is at the roots of both communism and socialism. He was the founder of the International Workingmen's Association, which was the forerunner of the world's Communist and Social Democratic parties. East Germany today considers itself a Marxist state. And Marxism, though much watered down and modified, was the underlying philosophy of the Social Democratic party which came to power in West Germany in 1969.

In 1848 Marx, together with his friend Friedrich Engels, the son of a wealthy German textile manufacturer, wrote the *Communist Manifesto* and launched the political movement that today governs a third of the people on earth.

That was also the year in which Europe was shattered by a series of revolutions. Some of them were social in nature, demanding more freedoms, economic improvements, and more rights for the workers. Others were of a largely nationalistic character, aimed at achieving independence from

44

foreign rule and at the creation of unified national states.

All these factors—economic freedom, social reform, political reform, and national unity—played a role in the revolution that struck the Germanys in 1848. But it was the concept of national union and the creation of a new German empire, to be governed by a kaiser who would have to answer to a democratically elected parliament, that became the dominant factor. The revolutionaries for the most part were liberal, democratic-minded intellectuals and idealistic noblemen, though a number of Marxists, including Engels, also played a significant role. In March 1848 their leading representatives, from all German states, met in St. Paul's Church in Frankfurt to draft a constitution for a new German empire.

Austria immediately insisted that if it joined this democratic empire it would have to be its dominant member. This the deputies to the Frankfurt Parliament could not accept. What they wanted was an empire made up of equals in which none of the thirty-nine German kingdoms, duchies, and principalities would play a dominant role. Unable to accept the Austrian conditions, they opted for a mini-Germany, that is, an empire without Austria and instead offered the imperial crown to the King of Prussia, who turned it down.

Not that Frederick William IV of Prussia did not want to become the emperor of a united Germany. On the contrary. But he was suspicious of the democratic and liberal attitudes of the Frankfurt Parliament. Moreover he too had strong ideas about dominating such a new empire. Prussia would not be satisfied with merely being the first among equals in a united empire. Within twenty-five years it was to get precisely what it wanted.

But in turning down the imperial crown, Prussia's king

took the wind out of the sails of the Frankfurt Parliament and the German revolutionary movement. The parliament was disbanded on orders of the various German dukes, princes, and kings, and the revolution itself, such as it was, crushed by troops of the ruler of the principality of Hesse, of which Frankfurt was the largest city. Some of the revolutionaries were imprisoned and many more were forced to flee. In fact more than a quarter million German liberals and intellectuals emigrated in 1849, the majority of them to the United States. One of them, Carl Schurz, became a founder of the Republican Party, campaigned for Abraham Lincoln in 1860, served as a Union general in the Battle of Gettysburg, represented Missouri as US Senator, and was Secretary of the Interior in the cabinet of President Rutherford B. Hayes.

The failure to create a liberal, democratic, constitutional German monarchy in 1848 was a tragedy. What came instead was a Prussian Germany based on arrogance, military power, and territorial expansion.

The die for the future was cast in 1862 when Otto von Bismarck, a brilliant but politically ruthless aristocrat, was appointed prime minister of Prussia. He was a man who once had advocated "blood and iron" as the solution to Germany's problems.

In 1864 he obtained Austria's support in a brief and successful war against little Denmark for control of the German-speaking regions of Schleswig-Holstein. Although Austria and Prussia agreed to administer the new territories jointly, within a year they had a falling out over how this should be done. In 1866 Prussia seized all of Schleswig-Holstein and a few weeks later also sent her troops in to occupy Saxony, Hanover, and Hesse. By then Prussia was so powerful and Austria so incensed that they went to war.

Otto von Bismarck, creator of the German Empire

The Austrian army was totally defeated at the Battle of Königgrätz.

Austria quit the German Confederation, leaving Prussia virtual master of the Germanys and free to create the "North German Federation," which was promptly joined by Bavaria, Württemberg, and the other southern German states.

This new alliance, with Prussia at the helm, was getting too powerful for the French. In July 1870, hoping for a showdown, Napoleon III declared war.

It was a short but bloody war in which the French fought gallantly. However, they were no match for the Prussians with their modern heavy armaments and brilliant tacticians. After six months it was all over. On January 18, 1871, the victorious German generals, politicians, kings, princes, dukes, and noblemen assembled in the Hall of Mirrors of Versailles Palace to hail the victor, Prussia's King Wilhelm I, and to proclaim him Kaiser of Germany. Bismarck was named the first German chancellor.

The Second Reich had been born. Austria was not a part of it. The kingdoms, especially Bavaria and Württemberg, retained a great amount of local independence and sovereignty, including the right to conduct foreign affairs, keep their own armies, currencies, and postal services. But it was an empire. It included Alsace-Lorraine, the traditional Middle Kingdom of Charlemagne's grandson, which the Prussians had annexed as war booty. In the east it stretched all the way to what was then Tsarist Russia.

The industrial age began and Germany, with its long tradition of trade and craftsmanship, prospered.

Bismarck was not only a skillful diplomat but an able administrator of domestic affairs. To cut the ground from under the feet of the growing Social Democratic, or socialist, party, he introduced the world's most advanced social

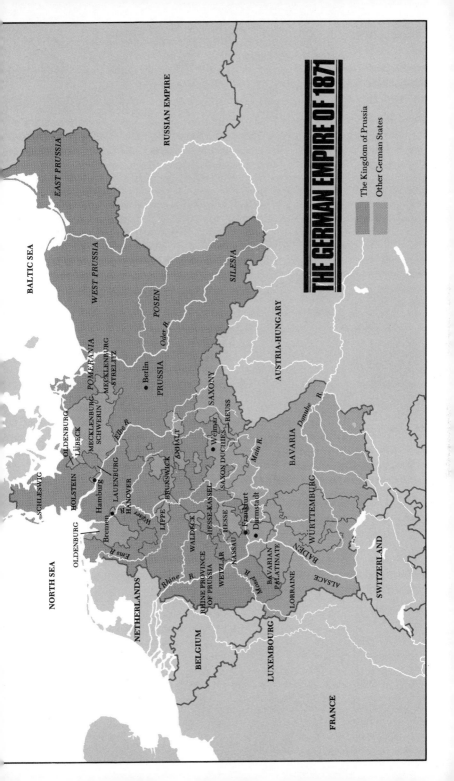

THE GERMAN EMPIRE OF 1871

The Kingdom of Prussia
Other German States

NORTH SEA

BALTIC SEA

SCHLESWIG

HOLSTEIN

OLDENBURG

OLDENBURG

LÜBECK

MECKLENBURG
SCHWERIN

MECKLENBURG
STRELITZ

POMERANIA

EAST PRUSSIA

WEST PRUSSIA

POSEN

SILESIA

PRUSSIA

• Berlin

Oder R.

RUSSIAN EMPIRE

Elbe R.

LAUENBURG

Hamburg •

Bremen

HANOVER

Weser R.

LIPPE

BRUNSWICK

ANHALT

• Weimar

SAXON DUCHIES

REUSS

SAXONY

Ems R.

WALDECK

HESSE-KASSEL

WETZLAR

HESSE

Frankfurt
• Darmstadt

Main R.

BAVARIA

Danube R.

WÜRTTEMBURG

NETHERLANDS

Rhine R.

RHINE PROVINCE
OF PRUSSIA

NASSAU

Moser R.

BADEN

AUSTRIA-HUNGARY

BELGIUM

LUXEMBOURG

BAVARIAN
PALATINATE

LORRAINE

ALSACE

SWITZERLAND

FRANCE

security system, which provided health and accident insurance, old-age pensions, and support payments for widows and orphans. Modernized and improved over the decades, it exists in both Germanys today and is still the most advanced in the world.

Theoretically, this powerful, prosperous new state in the center of Europe should have had a long, peaceful future. Bismarck had done his share to prepare it.

The future might have been peaceful had not Kaiser Wilhelm II come to the throne in 1888. He was arrogant, narrow-minded, and not too bright. He quarreled with Bismarck and fired him in 1890. Then he embarked on a risky, adventurous course. He created the most powerful army in Europe, which compelled a fearful France to enter into an alliance with Russia, a long-time foe. No sooner was the army ready than the kaiser proceeded to build a navy. This was a clear challenge to England, which then concluded an alliance with its traditional enemy, France. Germany was isolated with only Austria and Italy as its friends. The ground for World War I had been prepared.

Germany did not start the war. In fact it has been said that everyone started it, for Europe was so bored with itself in 1914 that it attempted suicide. But Germany got the blame and it waged a war so ruthless, so obviously motivated by lust for conquest and power that it became the principal enemy.

That war was the bloodiest and most devastating Europe had ever known. When it finally ended with an armistice on November 11, 1918, Germany, once so proud and mighty, had been broken.

Two days before the armistice, civil revolutions broke out in most of Germany. The kaiser abdicated, as did the kings of Bavaria, Württemberg, and Saxony. The nobility was abolished. Friedrich Ebert, the leader of the Social Democratic party, the largest in the German parliament, was proclaimed president of a new German republic. The second German empire had not lasted fifty years.

For a while it looked as if the new republic might not last fifty days. The Communist Spartacists—who had broken from the Social Democratic party during the war because the party had voted for the appropriations with which to fight it—were determined to turn Germany into a Soviet state like that which had been proclaimed in Russia. Everywhere in Germany "soldiers' and workers' councils,"—that is, *soviets*—began assuming power. Until mid-January 1919 all signs pointed to a Communist victory in Germany. Then the two leading Spartacists, Karl Liebknecht and Rosa Luxemburg, were murdered during a week of bloody fighting between Communists and army troops in Berlin. As soon as the fighting was over elections were held for a National Assembly, which would draw up a constitution for the new republic.

Two crucial documents drafted in 1919 were to shape the future of modern Germany. One was the Treaty of Versailles that ended the war. The other was the Weimar Constitution.

The Germans called the treaty "the most unjust in history, unbearable and unrealizable, intolerable for any nation." That is an overstatement. One can only speculate what kind of treaty the kaiser would have imposed had he won the war. But it was unfair and what was worse it was unwise, for it bore within it the seeds of the next world war. It placed all blame on Germany.

Under the terms of Versailles, drawn up by the United States, Great Britain, France, and Italy, Germany lost a tenth of its population, one-eighth of its territory, all of its overseas colonies, most of its iron ore deposits, and a good deal of its coal. Territories which Prussia had annexed in the eighteenth century were ceded to Poland. Part of Schleswig was returned to Denmark and all of Alsace-Lorraine to France. The Saarland was placed under French administration for fifteen years; the Rhineland was declared a permanently demilitarized zone and placed under American-British-French occupation.

The treaty restricted the German army to 100,000 men, prohibited it from having planes or tanks, and reduced the navy to little more than a token force.

Moreover Germany was ordered to pay reparations to France, Great Britain, and the other allies. The exact amount was to be determined later, but as a beginning $5 billion plus deliveries of coal, ships, lumber, and cattle were due between 1919 and 1921.

Any government would have been hard-pressed trying to fulfill those obligations. But for the new German government, created by the constitutional convention in Weimar, it was an impossible burden.

It not only made governing extremely difficult, but the new government was blamed for the hated treaty itself. As a result, the treaty sealed that government's fate before it was properly born.

The Weimar Constitution, which borrowed the best ideas of democracy from the laws of America, England, France, and Switzerland, was the most liberal and most perfectly democratic document the world had seen. But the Germans were not ready for it. The majority pined for the good old days of the monarchy when to be German meant being somebody in the world. They believed that Germany had not really lost the war on the battlefield but had been "stabbed in the back" on the home front. When the demands of the Versailles Treaty caused economic hardship, what was easier than to pin blame on the republic and democracy itself?

In this kind of atmosphere extremists had an easy time. For the first four years or so the Weimar Republic was full of extremists. They railed and ranted. The louder they shouted the worse things got. By November 1923 inflation was so rampant people had to carry basketsful of worthless paper money to the bakery to buy a loaf of bread. A mug of beer cost 43 billion marks, a newspaper 12 billion, and one American dollar was worth 418 billion.

There were numerous *putsches*—that is, attempts to take over legally established governments by force. In the provinces of Saxony and Thuringia, for example, the Communists took over the governments briefly. And on November 8, 1923, a man named Adolf Hitler almost succeeded in taking over that of Bavaria by kidnapping its three top officials at gunpoint in a Munich beer hall auditorium. From there he intended to march on Berlin with his private army of storm troopers to make himself master of all of Germany.

Hitler, who had been born in Braunau, an Austrian village close to the German border, was thirty-four years old at the time. He had tried his hand, unsuccessfully, as an artist in Vienna before World War I and had settled in Munich in 1913. With the outbreak of the war he enlisted in the Bavarian army. Returning to Munich after the armistice in 1918, he soon became involved in the radical, right-wing, nationalist movement that was flourishing in the city. He joined a tiny group called the National Socialist German Workers' party (the Nazi party), gained control of it, turned it into a paramilitary organization, and won the support of prominent nationalists including General Erich von Ludendorff, one of the great heroes of the German army in

53

World War I. It was with Ludendorff that he staged the Beer Hall Putsch and it was with Ludendorff that he intended to make himself master of Germany in 1923.

The Beer Hall Putsch was crushed in the same night it began by the army and the police. Hitler and Ludendorff were arrested and tried. By the end of 1923 economic stability had been restored to Germany and the inflation had been controlled. In 1925 Field Marshal von Hindenburg, the greatest hero of World War I, was elected president and the fledgling German Republic was on the way to recovery.

The German experiment with democracy might have succeeded, despite all the efforts to destroy it from within, had it not been for the world financial and economic crisis of 1929. The depression caused proportionally more unemployment and misery in Germany than elsewhere.

As economic chaos returned and a succession of administrations failed to cope with it, Hitler, whose Nazi party had been virtually disbanded after the Beer Hall Putsch, made a startling comeback. His message was simple if distorted. The Communists, the Socialists, the French, the British, and above all, the Jews were responsible for Germany's troubles. Everybody except the Germans. The nation needed hope and it needed scapegoats. Hitler provided both. That he mouthed mainly lies and false promises hardly mattered. They sounded good.

In January 1933 his Nazi party was so powerful and popular, and the country was in such disarray, that Hindenburg, the aging president, appointed Hitler chancellor and head of a coalition government.

Within a year Hitler had used his powers to destroy democracy and to turn Germany into a dictatorship. The constitution was suspended. Other political parties were outlawed, their leaders imprisoned in concentration camps.

Adolf Hitler gives the now-famous Nazi salute.

Books were burned. The Jews, whom Hitler had hated since his days as a poor artist in Vienna and who provided that convenient scapegoat, were hounded. Catholic and Protestant ministers were muzzled. Parliament was turned into a rubber-stamp body. It was a tyrannical regime in which the Gestapo (the secret police) and Hitler's storm troopers ruled with an iron fist.

It was the most dictatorial, most regimented, most uniform regime the world had ever seen. Those who swam with the tide and approved of the Fuehrer—or Leader, as Hitler called himself—prospered. Those who resisted or objected were soon crushed, for Hitler allowed no one the freedom to disagree with him. Freedom of the press and expression were abolished. The judiciary became a pliable tool in the hands of his Nazi party, doing its bidding in violation of all basic laws.

But Hitler also provided jobs. He built up a new army in violation of the Versailles Treaty. When he also promised the German people revenge for the humiliation of Versailles, renewed glory, and renewed greatness, he won the overwhelming support of the masses.

Hitler promised to create a new Thousand-Year Empire, the Third German Reich, and wasted no time pursuing his goals. Having gobbled up Austria, the Sudetenland, Bohemia, and Moravia, he touched off World War II by invading Poland. At the height of his power he ruled over more territory than had Napoleon and seemed on the verge of creating an empire bigger than Rome's. It reached from the Atlantic to deep in the heart of Russia, from the Arctic Circle to North Africa.

But like so many conquerors before him, Hitler had bitten off more than he could chew. The fortunes of war turned against him. The combined might of Russia, which he had invaded in 1941, and the United States, which Hitler's ally, Japan, had drawn into the war with the attack on Pearl Harbor in December 1941, was too much for the German army. In four years of bitter fighting the empire was rolled back until Russian and American troops met at the Elbe River in the middle of Germany, and the Allies, including the British and French, occupied the country.

Hitler's war, Germany's war, was the most devastating in human history. More than fifty million people were killed, among them six million Jews who were systematically and deliberately murdered in the German death camps.

When peace finally came to Europe in May 1945, Germany lay in ruins, its dreams of empire dashed forever. The Reich that Hitler promised would last a thousand years had endured just a little more than twelve.

3
To Conquer and Divide

On October 22, 1944, as the Allied and Soviet armies were closing in on Germany, a closely guarded Royal Air Force transport lifted from the runway at Moscow Airport and headed toward London. On board was Britain's Prime Minister Winston Churchill who had just spent two weeks talking about the postwar future with Josef Stalin, the Soviet dictator. From the plane Churchill sent a coded radio message summing up the conference to President Franklin D. Roosevelt in the White House.

"We also discussed informally the future partition of Germany," Churchill reported. "Contrary to his [Stalin's] previously expressed view, he would be glad to see Vienna as the capital of a federation of South German States including Austria, Bavaria, Württemberg, and Baden.

58

"As you know, the idea of Vienna becoming the capital of a large Danubian federation has always been attractive to me, though I should prefer to add Hungary, to which U.J. [Uncle Joe Stalin] is strongly opposed . . . U.J. wants Poland, Czechoslovakia, and Hungary to form a realm of independent, anti-Nazi, pro-Russian states.

"As to Prussia," Churchill continued, "U.J. wished the Ruhr and Saar detached and out of action, probably under international control, and a separate state formed in the Rhineland. He would also like the internationalization of the Kiel Canal. I am not opposed to this line of thought. However, you may be sure that we came to no fixed conclusions pending the triple meeting."

Of course, the Big Three had talked about it before. But surprising as it may sound, Churchill's cable to Roosevelt was the closest the leaders of America, Britain, and Russia ever came to seriously discussing Germany's division or what to do with the country after the war. What happened subsequently was that the big powers played it by ear. They had no plan and they allowed chance and inaction to dictate the course of history.

For example at the Triple Meeting, the famous Yalta Conference in February 1945, Stalin merely asked Churchill when he was going to make up his mind about the future of the Reich. "Since we are dealing with the fate of 80 million people," Churchill replied, "I think we need more time than 80 minutes to decide it." He suggested turning the question over to a "Dismemberment Committee" and Stalin agreed.

That committee never really got to work. By the time the war in Europe had ended in May, Roosevelt, who had advocated partition of Germany in 1943, was dead, and Stalin, who had also been for division at one point, had changed his mind.

Churchill, Roosevelt, and Stalin meet at Yalta, 1945.

When the Big Three, who now included the new American president, Harry S Truman, met again in Potsdam near Berlin in July 1945, they could not even agree on a definition for Germany. "The Germany of 1937," Truman suggested during one of the meetings. "What she has become after the war," said Stalin, insisting that the country no longer existed.

But the conference did agree that Poland was to get the territories east of the Oder-Neisse and to share East Prussia with the Soviet Union. The Sudetenland was restored to Czechoslovakia. The rest of the country was to be divided into four occupation zones, whose demarcation lines had been drawn on the map in London the previous September. They were to be administered by a four-power, Berlin-based Allied Control Council made up of the American, British, French, and Soviet military governors.

The four occupation zones would be treated as one economic unit and a "central German administration" was to run the economy and carry out the orders of the Control Council. There was no long-term plan, no concept for the future of Germany, though for all intents and purposes it was to remain unified.

Stalin went on record committing himself to that principle, and despite many claims to the contrary, supported it almost to his death in 1953. He counted on a relatively short period of occupation from which a completely de-Nazified, militarily weak, economically dependent but politically unified Germany would emerge.

All the evidence indicates that he did not want this unified Germany to be Communist. He was afraid of a unified Communist Germany with its tradition as the historical fountain and ideological cradle of Marxism. Such a Germany, Stalin feared, might some day play a more important role in the world than the USSR, and for a number of years he went to a lot of effort to prevent German Communists from creating it.

Nevertheless, despite the Allies' intentions at Potsdam, within a few years Germany was well on the way toward division. Why?

One reason was the absence of long-term policies and the weakness of the Allied Control Council, in which each military governor had a veto right. Each occupying power treated its zone like a personal preserve on which it imposed its own social and political views and its own ideas of doing things. Those ideas differed sharply, even between allies as alike as the Americans and the British.

The case of what happened to Konrad Adenauer is a perfect example. Adenauer had been mayor of his native Cologne until the Nazis came to power in 1933 and deposed him. In late March 1945, when the Americans occupied the Rhineland, they reinstated him. He established excellent relations with the US military government officers and they worked well together, trying to restore life to the devastated city. In June the Americans left, because Cologne was part of the British occupation zone, and British officers took over. They had a completely different way of doing things. Conflicts between them and Adenauer arose within a few days. The biggest one was over the trees in Cologne's parks and the "green belt" around the city which the British wanted cut down to provide firewood. Adenauer refused, arguing that they would not help to keep the people warm and were a long-term investment in the city's future. The British military governor fired him as mayor.

Just as the Americans and British sent Washington and London-trained German émigrés and administrators to their zones with the intent of remaking their areas in American and British images, so the Russians sent in Moscow-trained German Communists with the same aim. While the Western allies worked with liberal and conservative democratic politicians in their zones, the Russians naturally preferred the company of Communists and Socialists. While free enterprise and private farming were supported in the West, the Soviets encouraged land reform and nationalization of industry in the East.

But the greatest obstacle to preserving unity was posed by the French. France had entered the German occupation government at the last minute when its leader, General Charles de Gaulle, insisted on getting a cut of the spoils of war. Reluctantly the other three victors agreed. But France had been invited to the Potsdam Conference and its zone of occupation was carved out of the British and American ones as an afterthought. France, therefore, did not feel itself bound to the agreements reached at Potsdam.

De Gaulle offered all kinds of plans for annexing various parts of Germany such as the Rhineland, the Ruhr, and the Saar to France. His proposals met with stiff opposition from the US, Great Britain, and the USSR and were never realized, although he did annex the Saar for all practical purposes and it remained a part of France until 1955.

Meanwhile the French also refused to have anything to do with a unified administration of Germany and vetoed all moves in that direction in the Allied Control Council. French opposition during the autumn and winter of 1945 contributed significantly to the subsequent division of Germany.

A far more important cause, however, was the Cold War. Roots of mutual distrust between Russia and Britain and the US reached all the way back to the Russian Revolution of 1917. The Russians would never forget how the British and Americans had intervened in Russia on the anti-Communist side from 1918 to 1920. And most Americans and Britons distrusted the Russians and feared that they wanted to spread Communist revolution throughout the world.

During the 1930s the Russians remained very skeptical of Anglo-American intentions because they were convinced that US and British money had financed Hitler on his path to power. They believed that the Western capitalist countries were in cahoots with Germany. But in 1939, when Hitler and Stalin suddenly signed a friendship treaty, it was London's and Washington's turn to worry. They were even more worried when, immediately after Hitler invaded Poland, Stalin invaded from the other side and swallowed up those parts which Hitler had not conquered. When the Soviet Union waged war against Finland and occupied the three little Baltic republics of Lithuania, Latvia, and Estonia, it became hard to tell who the bigger aggressor in Europe was.

Not until the Germans invaded the Soviet Union in 1941 did Russia, Britain, and America decide to let bygones be bygones and to form the great coalition that defeated Germany. But it was never much more than a marriage of convenience and the first crack in it showed even before the war was over.

That was the so-called Bern incident when the Russians learned that German generals in Bern, Switzerland, were secretly negotiating the German surrender in Italy with British and American representatives. The Soviet leaders became convinced that the Allies intended to make a separate peace with Germany that would take the pressure off the German army and permit it to throw its weight against the Russians on the Eastern Front. Some German leaders were indeed hoping for this.

Much of the Cold War was based on misunderstandings —like the Bern incident—of who had promised what and who intended to do what to whom.

The Russians, who had been invaded four times by the West within a twenty-seven-year period, were determined to make sure it would not happen a fifth time. They had to remain strong, skeptical of everyone, and they wanted to create a protective buffer zone of friendly countries. All the countries in this zone—Poland, Czechoslovakia, Hungary, Romania, and Bulgaria—had been more or less unfriendly and anti-Communist in the years between the two world wars. Some, like Poland, had been Russia's enemies for centuries. It followed only naturally that for Russia to consider them friendly would also mean their being pro-Communist. As the Red Army marched through them, driving the Germans back, it left behind local and Moscow-trained Communists who eventually established pro-Soviet puppet governments. Of course Stalin considered all this perfectly legitimate and was even convinced that he had obtained Churchill's and Roosevelt's approval. Indeed Churchill had given Stalin a "free hand" in Bulgaria and Romania in exchange for which Stalin had promised the British a "free hand" in Greece.

The US saw this Soviet thrust into Europe in a completely different light.

First of all President Truman knew next to nothing of the agreements that had been made between Roosevelt, Churchill, and Stalin and therefore tended to see what the Russians were doing as naked aggression.

Secondly America, which had come out of the war the

most powerful nation on earth, had a deep sense of mission. It believed it had fought the war to free the world of dictatorship and wanted very much to bring the "American Way of Life" to all countries. Though this was a noble goal, US policy failed to take into account that some of those countries had a completely different tradition. American leaders objected, with justification, that the puppet governments created by Moscow in Eastern Europe and the Balkans were not democratic, forgetting all the time that, except for Czechoslovakia, these countries had never been democracies and did not know what democracy really meant.

Thirdly the United States misread both Stalin's intentions and his character. Of course he was a cruel, tyrannical dictator, but during the wartime alliance when he was cheerfully called Uncle Joe, America preferred not to think of him that way. When the war was over and some of Stalin's crimes were remembered, people in the US immediately assumed that like some other recent cruel dictators, Stalin must also be a world conquerer. But not all dictators have world conquest on their minds and Stalin was one of those who did not.

Finally although the US had no evil intentions whatsoever, it had a monopoly on the atomic bomb, the world's most fearful weapon, which upset the balance of power and frightened the Russians. When the USSR failed to disarm and demobilize its army as quickly and completely as America did, Washington read this as proof of Soviet military designs on Western Europe. Actually the Russians were afraid of atomic America and kept their army to protect themselves.

These were the principal causes of the Cold War on which billions of dollars and billions of rubles were spent for weapons and propaganda, to buy friends, influence people, and to try to prove one system better than the other.

Germany, where the two Super Powers stood face to face like wrestlers poised to lunge, was in the middle of it all.

The first real break between the Americans and Russians was over the question of German reparations.

The Soviets had specified their demands at the Yalta Conference in February 1945 where they proposed that Germany be made to pay reparations of $20 billion, half of this amount to go to the Soviet Union, which had suffered the most during the war. Payment was to be made in goods and property, rather than cash. No one questioned the USSR's need for reparations to help postwar reconstruction. Nor was the Soviet demand out of line. In fact, the amount the Russians wanted was lower than Western estimates of actual Soviet losses. But Roosevelt and Churchill were lukewarm to the whole idea, doubting whether such huge amounts could be taken out of the German economy. The US, especially, was opposed to any plan for which it might eventually have to pay by helping to keep the Germans from starving. The issue was shelved at Yalta and no amount was ever agreed upon, although the Russians as well as the British and Americans more or less took $10 billion as the Soviet share for granted.

At the Potsdam Conference agreement was reached that reparations should be handled on a zonal basis, each victor taking for himself what he needed and wanted from his zone. To compensate the Soviets for the lack of industrial facilities in their zone, the US and UK agreed to turn over to the Russians 10 per cent of the industrial equipment confiscated in the American and British zones. An additional 15 per cent of the British and American zones' production would be given to the Soviets, in exchange for which the

USSR was to deliver food and raw materials of equal value from its zone. Moreover each occupation power agreed to keep the others informed of its reparations and dismantling policy.

The plan was based on the false assumption that Germany would be treated as an economic whole. Actually, each occupying power went its own way. The French refused to cooperate at all. The Americans and British were reluctant about reparations because they remembered how badly the reparations policy had worked after World War I. The Soviets began by dismantling just about everything that could be moved.

Nearly 2,000 East German plants were entirely or partly dismantled and sent to Russia. More than 1,600 miles of railway line were completely torn out and on an additional 7,300 miles the parallel tracks were ripped up. Railway freight cars, automobiles, trucks, 1.2 million wood ties, the equipment of thirteen airports and three radio stations went to the USSR. Whatever the Russians could not dismantle they turned into 200 Soviet-owned companies whose output was geared entirely to meet reparations demands.

By the terms of the Potsdam Treaty that was all perfectly legitimate. But the Russians, like the French, failed to inform the British and Americans what they were doing. Nor did they deliver food or raw materials to the Western zones. On the contrary they sent around "reparations commissions" to select additional industrial equipment to be dismantled.

This led to numerous clashes. In Berlin in January 1946, for example, Soviet and American officials tangled when the Russians attempted to confiscate twelve locomotives being used in the railroad yard of the city's American sector.

"We just couldn't go on that way," wrote General

Lucius D. Clay, the US military governor. "Soviet practice meant that the US and Britain were paying, indirectly, for deliveries to Russia. When my repeated warnings brought no results, I decided to halt deliveries from our zone."

That, as Clay admitted many years later, was the "beginning of the split."

In May 1946 Clay recommended a halt to all forms of reparations and suggested helping the Germans to rebuild to prevent economic chaos and political disorders. In September James F. Byrnes, then the American secretary of state, speaking in Stuttgart, announced that "America is for the economic unity of Germany, but if we cannot obtain complete unity then we are for the greatest amount of unity we can get."

At the beginning of 1947 the British and Americans merged their two zones into what became known as Bizonia. That was as much unity as anyone was likely to get for a while.

The arguments over reparations continued for most of 1947. As the Russians became more stubborn, the US and Britain moved toward closer cooperation between themselves and with the Germans in their zones. By December 1947, when the four foreign ministers met in London for one of their regular conferences, an open break seemed unavoidable. Vyacheslav Molotov, the Soviet representative, delivered an insulting attack against the US, claiming that America had enriched itself during the war, while Russia had suffered at the hands of the Germans.

The gap continued to grow during the next months.

The dispute began to focus on a currency reform for Germany. Although the Russians agreed to a monetary reform in principle, they insisted on printing all the notes, for which the old plates were in Soviet hands. The British and

Americans, fearing they would have no control over the amount of new money if the Russians were to print it, refused to go along with this. By March 1948 the argument became so heated that the Soviet military governor walked out of the Allied Control Council, which at that time was the closest thing Germany had to a government.

The Americans and British were determined to go ahead with currency reform even without the Russians. New money was hurriedly printed on newly designed plates in America. After persuading the French to go along with it, this money was introduced as the only legal currency in the three western zones on June 20, 1948. That was the *Deutsche mark,* which has become one of the strongest currencies in the world today.

Germany had two currencies and the Russians were furious. They announced that the new Western money would not be allowed in Berlin, which they said is "within the Soviet occupation zone and is economically part of the Soviet zone." With that the Soviets challenged the Western powers' right to do in their sectors of Berlin what they pleased. The Americans, British, and French refused to bow to the Soviet edict and introduced the new money in West Berlin as well. The Russians replied by printing their own new money and by blocking off Western access to Berlin over the land routes that ran through the Soviet Zone.

Thus began the "Berlin Blockade" which the Western Allies broke successfully, after nearly eleven months, with the "Berlin Airlift." During the airlift American transport planes made 277,728 flights to the city, bringing West Berliners more than two million tons of coal, foodstuffs, raw materials, and medicine.

*Children in West Berlin watch an arriving plane
bring supplies during the 1948 Berlin Airlift.*

During the summer of 1948 the French finally agreed that their zone should join with the American and British in a single economic and political unit. At the same time the Western military governors began prodding local German leaders and politicians to form a separate West German government.

In September 1948 a Parliamentary Council met in Bonn to draw up a democratic federal constitution. The document was completed in May 1949 and soon approved by the military governors. In August elections were held to a federal parliament, the *Bundestag.* The strongest party turned out to be that of Konrad Adenauer's Christian Democratic Union (CDU), and when the new parliament met in September 1949 he was chosen the new federal chancellor —that is, prime minister. Although the new government's powers were still restricted, the Federal Republic of Germany (FRG) was born—as a separate state. Its capital, by a narrow choice, became Bonn.

The Russians had been watching developments in the West carefully. When it appeared obvious that a separate government would be created, they began doing the same.

A German People's Council was formed to draw up a constitution, and on October 7, 1949, the German Democratic Republic (GDR) was proclaimed. Its predominant political party was the Socialist Unity party (SED), which had been created in 1946 by fusing the Communists and the Social Democrats in the Soviet Zone—much to the objection of the Social Democrats in the Western zones. The party's leader, Walter Ulbricht, became the real power behind the scenes, although a former Social Democrat, Otto Grotewohl, was named the GDR's first prime minister and Wilhelm Pieck, an aging veteran Communist, its first president.

Germany was formally divided into two countries.

Officially both were committed to the idea of one Germany and for many years their leaders as well as the leaders of the four occupation powers continued to give lip service to that idea. But in practice the two Germanys kept drifting further and further apart.

As the Cold War widened, the rift between the US and the USSR grew. So did the gap between the two Germanys which they had created.

In 1950, after the start of the war in Korea, the US became increasingly concerned about Europe's ability to defend itself. A European Defense Community with a West European army was proposed. West Germany was supposed to join it and provide 150,000 men. This appealed to Adenauer, who saw in it a means for West Germany to gain her sovereignty and to win the respect of the Western world. For the next few years the headlines in Europe were dominated by the idea of this multinational force against supposed Soviet aggression. The whole scheme was finally abandoned in 1954 when the French parliament voted against it. Instead West Germany became part of NATO (North Atlantic Treaty Organization). But in the meantime it had won in prestige and was being integrated into Western Europe.

The plans to rearm West Germany as part of the Western alliance shocked the Russians. Nothing worried Stalin more than the prospect of a remilitarized Western Germany. To forestall this, he proposed the withdrawal of occupation troops from all four zones of Germany, free elections, German reunification, and a small independent military force for Germany in exchange for a unified Germany's complete neutrality. That March 1952 offer, to judge from information that has become available since then, was made in all seriousness. However, neither the Western Allies nor West Germany ever took him up on it.

A year later, after Stalin's death in March 1953, there was another Soviet offer from some of Stalin's successors, notably Lavrenti Beria, the powerful chief of the Soviet secret police. Beria was locked in a power struggle with Georgi Malenkov and Nikita Khrushchev, the two other top leaders who had survived Stalin. Beria hoped to beat them out of the running by coming to terms with America and Britain. He was prepared to sacrifice East Germany and Ulbricht in exchange.

Throughout April, May, and early June of 1953 Beria pressed strongly for a settlement. His private emissaries were in touch with Churchill. His secret henchmen had gone to East Germany to secure the support of more liberal and flexible men within the East German leadership for a political coup against Ulbricht.

Beria's ploy might have worked had fate not intervened on Ulbricht's behalf. Worried by loosening discipline after Stalin's death, possibly tipped off about Beria's plans, and determined to build up a strong Communist East Germany that would be too valuable for the Russians to sell down the river, Ulbricht used the spring of 1953 to try to pull the GDR up by its own bootstraps. One of his techniques was to raise the work norms, that is, to compel people to work even harder than before for the same pay. By June 16 pressure on the labor force was so great that construction workers in East Berlin started demonstrating for a relaxation of the new work norms. Their demonstration soon turned into a nationwide rebellion against the government that the Russian occupation forces had no choice but to crush with tanks and guns on June 17. When the revolt was over, Ulbricht was more firmly in the saddle than ever before and

Beria's plotters within the East German leadership had been exposed. Before the month was over Beria himself was arrested by Malenkov and Khrushchev in the Kremlin, brought to trial, and executed.

Whether or not a great opportunity for German reunification was missed in the spring of 1953 remains one of the great "ifs" of postwar history. At any rate for the next twenty years almost no other opportunity presented itself.

In May 1955, a decade after VE Day, the occupation of the three Western zones was ended formally. West Germany became an independent, sovereign power and joined NATO as a full-fledged member with the obligation to put up an army of nearly 500,000 men.

The USSR replied by declaring East Germany also sovereign and by creating the Warsaw Pact organization of which the GDR became a member.

West Germany's policy for the next fifteen years or so was based on the hope of reunifying Germany by absorbing East Germany into the Federal Republic, and of course, dissolving the East Berlin government. For years the Federal Republic denied the GDR's existence and insisted that it ruled and represented the 17 million people of East Germany as well. Bonn contended that there could be only one Germany and that it was this sole Germany. To enforce this policy in foreign affairs it devised the "Hallstein Doctrine," named after Walter Hallstein, one of its senior diplomats. The doctrine required the Federal Republic to break diplomatic relations with and deny recognition to any country having diplomatic ties with East Germany.

East Germany's answer to the Hallstein Doctrine was the "Ulbricht Doctrine," which barred recognition of all countries that in any way supported West Germany's claim to be the only legal German state.

The more one hard-headed doctrine collided with the other, the more relations between the two Germanys worsened and chances for reunification evaporated.

During those years the creators and champions of the two Germanys, the United States and the Soviet Union, continued to pay lip service to the idea of eventual reunification. But lip service was all it really was. Although the original occupation policy had been dedicated to the principal of maintaining unity, once the two Germanys began their recovery and developed into powerful states in their own right, reunification no longer seemed such an appealing idea. The prospect of a powerful, reunited Germany in the heart of Europe—capitalist, communist, or neutral— could hardly arouse much enthusiasm in the US, in the USSR, or among the other European states. Memories of both world wars and Germany's rule in them were too fresh. Many people in America as well as in Russia felt strongly that division was merely a fair price that Germany should pay for the war.

Nor were Germans and their leaders as committed to the idea of reunification as they wanted their constituents and the outside world to believe. No election campaign could be waged, no political rally staged in either Germany without all manner of candidates and public officials proclaiming their everlasting dedication to the goal of German unity. No doubt many of them even believed their own promises and propaganda. But in practice they frequently pursued a different line, one that served to perpetuate the division of the country.

4
Four Germans

Although Konrad Adenauer was a true-blooded Rhine-
lander, a native of Cologne and of King Lothair's Middle
Kingdom, he looked oriental—somewhat like an American
Indian chief with almond-shaped eyes that seemed constantly to be scanning the far horizon; very high cheek-
bones; a leathery skin marked by deep lines and scars
caused by an automobile accident; a ramrod-straight figure.
But it was more than just looks. There was a calm about
him, an aura of shrewdness, wisdom, righteousness, aus-
terity, and stamina that could have come right off the Central Asian plateau or the American prairies.

His admirers compared him with Bismarck. And even his
political enemies grudgingly and respectfully called him
Der Alte—The Old One.

His life, from 1876 until 1967, spanned the most tragic and tumultuous century in German history. It also covered four distinct eras. Born into Bismarck's Second Empire, Adenauer was named mayor of Cologne in 1917 and was already middle-aged and a well-known politician when the last kaiser abdicated in 1918. During the fourteen years of the Weimar Republic he played an important, though not decisive role as mayor of Germany's fourth largest city and as one of the leaders of the influential Catholic Center party. Adenauer sat out the third period, Hitler's Nazi Reich, in enforced retirement, and for a while, as a political prisoner. The fourth era opened with Adenauer almost 70, but he did more to shape and influence it than any other German.

There are those who say that if Adenauer, who came close to being named chancellor of the Weimar Republic in 1921 and again in 1926, had been permitted to shape that second era as well, the third and fourth might never even have happened, for history would have taken a completely different course.

There are also those who claim that without Adenauer the fourth period might not have been marked by Germany's division and the existence of two Germanys.

Both statements contain more than a grain of truth.

After 1945 Konrad Adenauer proved to be one of the toughest, shrewdest, and most brilliant politicians of the twentieth century. As they watched him, people began to realize that although he was ruthless, stubborn, and not always entirely honest, Adenauer might have been the man, if there were one at all, who could have saved the Weimar Republic.

What had been needed in the 1920s was a man with the resilience, strength of character, and staying power to pre-

Konrad Adenauer

vent the chaos that paved the way for Hitler's take-over. Adenauer had those qualities.

During the first attempt to draft him as chancellor of Germany in 1921, Adenauer had laid down conditions that his sponsors and coalition partners refused to meet. One of these was his unpopular tax program, the other his intention to add an extra hour to the eight-hour working day in order to put Germany back on its feet economically. A less uncompromising man was chosen to run the government. Adenauer was approached and asked to form a government a second time in 1926, but again, when the chips were down in the smoke-filled rooms, the choice fell on a more pliable man. As one of Germany's leading newspapers said at the time, "It is a pity that an Adenauer government could not have been set up. The mayor of Cologne may be a difficult character, but at any rate he's *got* character."

History took its fateful course. Almost a quarter century passed before Adenauer got a third opportunity to form a German government. This time he grabbed it with both hands. In fact, the line-up of political parties in the new West German Bundestag was so close in September 1949 that Adenauer was elected chancellor with a majority of only one vote—his own.

Asked afterwards whether he had voted for himself, the crusty, clever old politician replied, "But of course. Anything else would have been hypocritical."

Adenauer was 73 when he was elected chancellor and his doctor pronounced him fit enough to carry on for two years. In fact, he remained chancellor for fourteen, and when he resigned in 1963 in the middle of his fourth term in office, he did so reluctantly and under pressure from his own Christian Democratic party, which could not stand his high-handed manner of running the country any more.

His achievements had been enormous. West Germany, his Germany, had regained the respect and admiration of the world. It had tried to atone for the crimes committed by the Third Reich by voluntarily paying out billions to its victims. It had made peace with Germany's age-old foe, France. It had a new army. It was on the way to becoming a reliable democracy. And it was by far the most prosperous and economically powerful country in Europe. But it was only half a Germany.

No one had identified himself more closely with the goal of German reunification than Adenauer. However, the record shows that he deliberately passed up several real chances to reunify Germany as a neutral country in order to keep the Federal Republic firmly allied with America, Western Europe, and NATO.

The reasons for his actions, which speak so much louder than his glowing words and promises, remain obscure. They were secrets he took to the grave with him at age 91 in 1967. But one cannot help speculating.

Adenauer had always had somewhat of a separatist streak in him plus a dyed-in-the-hide contempt for Prussia and Prussia's dominant role in the German Empire. On several occasions as mayor of Cologne in the 1920s he had toyed with the idea of creating a separate German Rhineland Republic. It would be Catholic in its religious orientation, pro-French, and Western in its foreign policy, free of domination by Protestant, eastward-looking Prussia.

Nothing ever came of these various schemes, but the idea lingered in his mind right through Nazi-enforced retirement from public life, and it was still there when he re-entered the political stage in 1945.

At that time he told an American journalist, "A Prussian is nothing but a Slav who has forgotten who his grandfather was."

In a newspaper interview in 1946 he said, "It is my belief that Germany's future capital should be situated in the southwest rather than in Berlin, far to the east. The new capital should lie somewhere in the region of the river Main, where Germany's windows are wide open to the West. If, on the other hand, Berlin becomes the capital once again, distrust of Germany abroad will become unavoidable. Whoever makes Berlin the new capital will be creating a new spiritual Prussia."

That the capital of his Germany ended up being Bonn, just fifteen miles upstream from his native Cologne and across the Rhine river from his mansion at Rhöndorf, was no accident.

Moreover Adenauer was a pragmatic politician who knew where the votes were and how to get them.

The conservative Christian Democratic party, which he had launched after World War II and which dominated German politics right until 1969, relied on the support of Catholics in the Rhineland and Bavaria and on conservative Protestant voters in other parts of the Federal Republic. Its margins of victory, however, were always small. In fact, Adenauer's party won a clear majority of the seats in the Bundestag only once—in 1957. The rest of the time it had pluralities and depended on the backing of other parties in parliament to form coalition governments.

On the other hand the area that now comprises East Germany had always been strongly Protestant and liberal and until 1930 this part of Germany had voted heavily socialist and communist.

Adenauer knew only too well that if the eastern part of

Germany were reunited with the western regions the balance of political power would shift against him and his Christian Democrats would be doomed forever to a minority, opposition role.

That may have been another reason why Adenauer talked a great deal about reunification but in practice made every effort to prevent it.

Similar thoughts may have motivated Walter Ulbricht, the one-time Leipzig carpenter who was the virtual ruler of East Germany for twenty-five years.

Like Adenauer, Ulbricht was born into Bismarck's Second Empire and his life spanned those four distinct eras of German history. He was born in a bleak tenement in Leipzig, the cradle of the German working-class movement, the son of a poor and frequently tipsy tailor and his pretty but sickly wife. Both parents were ardent militant Socialists and from birth fed him heaping spoonfuls of Marxism. He thrived on that diet and by the time he began school he already had been nicknamed "Red."

Like most German children of his class, Ulbricht left school at fourteen to learn a trade—cabinetmaking and carpentry. By 1912, when he was nineteen, he joined the Social Democratic party of which his father was a veteran member. His career in the party of his father was short. In 1914 when the party's Reichstag faction voted war appropriations to the kaiser, Ulbricht joined the antiwar, radical group of Karl Liebknecht and Rosa Luxemburg whose Spartacus League later became the German Communist party.

Ulbricht's rise in the Communist party, whose inaugural meeting he attended in 1919, was steady though unspectacular. He climbed the rungs of power through persistence, diligence, and cunning, not brilliance or flair. He was valued most for his talents as an organizer. For a while he studied at a party school in Moscow where he also met Lenin. Then he worked as a propagandist and Communist agent in Austria. In 1926 he entered the Saxonian state legislature as a Communist deputy. In 1928 he was elected on the Communist ticket to the Reichstag. By 1929 he was also the political boss of the Communist party in Berlin-Brandenburg and a top-ranking party official on the national scene.

After Hitler took power and the Communist party was outlawed in Germany Ulbricht fled. He worked for the *Comintern,* the Communist International, in Czechoslovakia, France, Spain, and Sweden, and arrived in Moscow in 1938. By then he was one of the leaders of the German Communist party in exile. When the Germans invaded the Soviet Union, Ulbricht took charge of attempts to "re-educate" German prisoners of war, serving as a Soviet army colonel.

On April 30, 1945, just a few hours before Adolph Hitler committed suicide in Berlin, Ulbricht and nine of his top aides boarded a Soviet DC-3 in Moscow to return to Germany after twelve years of exile. The "Ulbricht Group," as it was called, was attached to the headquarters of Soviet Marshal Georgi Zhukov near Berlin.

Ulbricht's instructions at the time went no further than to "assist Soviet military commandants in taking all necessary measures for normalizing the life of the German populace as quickly as possible," and there were no thoughts of making him a new German ruler. But on his arrival there was a prophetic slip of the tongue by one of the Russian officers who had come to meet Ulbricht's plane. "It is a special pleasure to greet you," said the Russian, "because we have heard that you are the members of the new German government."

Ulbricht soon began laying the groundwork for the Communist Germany he envisioned. The first and most important step was fusing the Social Democratic with his own Communist party to create the Socialist Unity party (SED), which rules the GDR today. Ulbricht was named the new party's chief. Like the chiefs of Communist parties elsewhere, including the USSR, he quickly became the most powerful figure in the Soviet occupation zone. Since the party is the fountain of all power, the government and state titles that Ulbricht acquired later were only trappings.

Twice during his reign there were attempts by rivals to unseat him. During the first one in 1953, which Beria sponsored from Moscow, the Berlin workers' uprising saved him. In 1958 he managed to neutralize his opponents in the party before they could topple him. Out of each crisis he emerged stronger, more powerful than before.

By the late 1960s Ulbricht was a respected elder statesman of the Communist world whose words and views carried a lot of weight in Moscow. He was, after all, practically the only political leader left in the Communist world who had met Lenin personally. And he was a man who had already been a leader of the German Communist party when men like Leonid Brezhnev and Alexei Kosygin were still in school or college.

On occasion Ulbricht talked glowingly of German reunification, just as Konrad Adenauer did. In 1946 he said, "Our people cannot exist without the unity of Germany. Saxony cannot live without the Ruhr and Bavaria cannot endure without Saxony." His aim, of course, was to make a reunified Germany a Communist one, for Ulbricht, sixteen years

Walter Ulbricht (left) *with Soviet
Premier Nikita Khrushchev*

younger than Adenauer, had been as active and prominent a Communist politician in pre-Hitler Germany as Adenauer had been a Catholic, conservative one. But Ulbricht also understood that the Communists would have little chance of coming to power legally in a reunified Germany. The Socialists—yes, they would make it. But not the Communists.

He decided that he would stick with the East German bird he had in hand. Ulbricht stopped talking about unity in the early 1960s and set out to build the most powerful and prosperous East Germany possible.

Ulbricht dominated the postwar German scene even longer than Adenauer and in many ways was an even more controversial politician. At the height of his power, when the wall was built in 1961, he was perhaps the most hated man in both Germanys. He was called a "puppet of Moscow" and the "Kremlin's henchman," a cunning tyrant, and unpatriotic bureaucrat of international Communism who had sold his people into slavery.

One of the bitterest political jokes of that period describes the devil knocking on the gates of heaven one day. "What do *you* want here?" asks St. Peter, looking out. "Ulbricht," Satan replies, "has just arrived in Hell, and I'm the first refugee."

By the time he died at age eighty in 1973, no longer chief of the Socialist Unity party but still nominally the GDR's president, Ulbricht's public image had changed radically. Even his bitterest opponents paid him grudging respect. "Ulbricht," said one of his sharpest West German critics, "was the most successful German politician since Bismarck."

There was a lot of truth in that. Ulbricht had beaten all the odds, had surmounted the most incredible difficulties and had proven all the predictions wrong. When he died, East Germany, his Germany, was a major industrial power in its own right, recognized diplomatically by most of the world's nations and on the threshhold of membership in the UN.

Although of completely different backgrounds, Ulbricht and Adenauer had a lot in common. Both were shrewd politicians with a remarkable ability to manipulate men. Both were stubborn and tough, and both were masters of the craft of using political power toward their own ends. Both lacked imagination and had an ingrained distrust of intellectuals. They were doers, not thinkers. Both were also provincial in their outlooks.

Because he looked so Asiatic, Adenauer was once asked in jest whether some of his ancestors might have come from the East. "Could be, could be," *Der Alte* replied in apparent seriousness. "I've heard that some of my forebears came from as far east as the Harz Mountains." The Harz Mountains, a range that straddles the border between East and West Germany, is about as far east as Adenauer's mind ranged. He looked West—toward France.

Ulbricht looked East—toward Poland and Russia. For him the Harz Mountains were an intellectual frontier long before they had become the boundary between his and Adenauer's Germanys. He regarded Adenauer's Rhineland and the Ruhr Basin as a nest of capitalist, monopolist throat-cutters, the home of traitors, exploiters of the working class, and modern robber barons.

Neither knew very much about the other's Germany, save what they had been told by aides and advisers, and in their hearts they were basically loyal to the Germanys in which they had been born.

Like Adenauer, Ulbricht had an unforgettable face and was a cartoonist's delight. With his balding head, gray mustache, pointed Lenin-style beard, rimless glasses perched schoolmasterly on his nose, his tightly buttoned suit jackets, and stiff-necked manners, he was his own best caricature. Yet in his narrow, humorless pale-blue eyes there was a glint which once prompted Clara Zetkin, the grand old lady of German communism, to say of Ulbricht, who sat next to her in the Reichstag, "May fate prevent him from ever rising to the top of the party. Look into his eyes and see how conniving and dishonest he is."

His voice was so squeaky, his accent so Saxonian, and his oratorical delivery so bad, it gave rise to what East Germans facetiously called a new unit of time—an "ulb." That is the time it takes for the first hand to reach out and switch off the set as soon as Ulbricht's voice comes over radio or TV.

His beard was the source of even more whispered jokes. One tells of Ulbricht's going for a haircut and falling asleep in the chair. When he wakes up he discovers the barber has also shaved off his beard. "Are you crazy?" Ulbricht screams. "That beard was the last piece of Leninism in our party."

But for all the ribbing it caused him, Ulbricht was never embarrassed by nor reluctant to talk about his goatee. "It was grown in the battle against Hitler," he told one interviewer. "Back in 1933 when the Nazis took power and we Communists went underground, I had to have a disguise to escape the Gestapo and I grew this beard. I am proud of it. Konrad Adenauer never grew a beard. He didn't have to. He was never a threat to the Nazis."

Like Adenauer, Ulbricht thrived on the Cold War. Like Adenauer's, Ulbricht's political importance began to wane as the Cold War subsided. And like Adenauer, or perhaps like all old men in politics and government who try to keep younger, fresher men from power, Ulbricht became increasingly stubborn in his old age. In 1971 when he put more and more obstacles in the path of Moscow's plans to come to terms with West Germany and to find a way for reducing Cold War tension, Ulbricht's rule was broken. The move to dump him was obviously started in Moscow; but by Communist standards it was the gentlest dumping of a party chief in history. Ulbricht kept his job as Chairman of the State Council, that is as East Germany's president, a largely honorary role, until his death. But Erich Honecker, his longtime deputy, replaced him as First Secretary of the Socialist Unity party.

In Erich Honecker Moscow obviously thought it had a much more pliable man. And during his first two years in office, Honecker was indeed quite responsive to Soviet pressure, especially in the field of foreign affairs. But Honecker, it soon turned out, was cut from a different mold than Ulbricht with ideas and a style of his own.

Age—he is almost a generation younger than Ulbricht—as well as origin and background have a lot to do with it.

Although Honecker was also raised in a militantly left-wing family, he is not, like Ulbricht was, a native East German. He is from the Saar, part of the old Middle Kingdom of Charlemagne's grandson Lothair, between the Rhine and France. For seventeen of the first twenty-three years of Honecker's life, his home town, Neunkirchen, was under French administration.

Born in 1912, the third of six children of a Socialist coal miner, Honecker was raised in a Marxist environment even more militant than Ulbricht's.

His father, who remained full of Communist brine and fury until his death at eighty-nine in 1969, had been one of the leaders of a bitter mine workers' strike in 1913 and was one of the first Saar Socialists to switch to the fledgling Communist party after World War I.

Honecker was raised on a diet of hunger and revolution. In his own accounts of his childhood he portrays a lively household in which revolutionaries, strikers, and Marxist agitators came and went. Lenin, Liebknecht, and Rosa Luxemburg were family idols. Conspiratorial whispering in the living room was the rule, not the exception. Honecker grew up believing that revolution "is fun."

By the time he was ten years old he was a member of the Communist party's children's organization, the Young Pioneers. He joined the Communist Youth League at fourteen and became a full-fledged party member four years later. In 1930 he went to Moscow for a year of training as a Communist Youth official and when he returned to the Saar in 1931, he became a full-time party and Youth League organizer. After Hitler came to power, he worked for a while with the exiled German Communist party leadership in France, but in 1935 he was ordered to go to Berlin to organize underground anti-Hitler resistance groups. He was caught by the Gestapo in February 1936. A Nazi court convicted him of attempted treason and sentenced him to ten years in Brandenburg penitentiary, from which he was liberated by Red Army troops in 1945.

His first postwar assignment was to organize the Free German Youth organization, East Germany's Communist Youth League, which he headed until 1955. Then Ulbricht sent him to Moscow for two more years of training. When Honecker returned in 1957 he moved into the inner circle of the East German leadership as a member of the party's Politburo and the man in charge of military, security, and counterintelligence affairs. By 1958 he was the number two man in the party and Ulbricht's designated successor.

Since taking over from Ulbricht in May 1971 Honecker has proven to be far more flexible, less dogmatic, and more

Erich Honecker, First Secretary of the Socialist Unity party

modern and progressive in his outlook than anyone would have predicted. His attitude seems to be: "Anyone who is not against us is for us." Though he does not carry the weight in Communist circles that Ulbricht did, he is trying to prove himself as the manager-leader of the world's most prosperous, modern, and efficient Communist state. He has surrounded himself with a number of younger leaders (including his wife Margot, the GDR's minister of education) who unlike members of Ulbricht's old team do not have their ideological roots in the Kaiser Reich or the Weimar Republic. Like Honecker himself they are men and women molded largely by the experience of Nazi and postwar divided Germany. Communism to them is less a political philosophy than a way of life, for it is under communism that they have made it. In every sense they are members of a different generation than either Ulbricht or Adenauer.

Willy Brandt, chancellor of West Germany from 1969 to May 1974, leader of the Social Democratic Party, and architect of the controversial *Ostpolitik,* has a lot in common with them.

Brandt, a year younger than Honecker, was not the direct successor to Adenauer, who resigned in 1963. Two chancellors, Ludwig Erhard and Kurt Georg Kiesinger, both Christian Democrats, preceded him before his Social Democratic party won enough votes in the 1969 election to form a governing coalition with the third party in the Bundestag, the Free Democrats. But Erhard and Kiesinger were Adenauer holdovers who attempted to pursue *Der Alte*'s policies in a different style. It fell upon Brandt to set the signals, change the switches, and plot out the new directions that have determined West Germany's course in the early 1970s.

Technically speaking, his name is neither Willy nor Brandt. That is a pen name he adopted as a writer and journalist to avoid Nazi persecution. He has adopted it legally and everybody calls him by that name today.

He was born in 1913 as Herbert Karl Frahm, the illegitimate son of a twenty-year-old shopgirl in Lübeck, where northern Germany's rolling hills make their peace with the Baltic Sea. It is a port and trading city of proud rebellion and class consciousness that has produced not only radicals but two of Germany's outstanding twentieth-century writers: Thomas and Heinrich Mann.

From both his mother and grandfather and later from his stepfather, Brandt inherited Social Democratic teachings. By the time he was nine years old, he was well aware of the difference between rich and poor, and that he was poor.

It was during a strike and his grandfather, a truck driver, was out of work. "Hunger," said Brandt in his autobiography, *My Road to Berlin,* "stood in the kitchen like an evil landlord." One day as he stared hungrily into the window of a bakery shop his striking grandfather's boss came by. He bought two loaves of bread for the boy. "I ran home out of breath," Brandt recalls. "Grandfather was very angry and told me to take the bread back. He said, 'A striker does not accept gifts from his employer. We will not let ourselves be bribed by our enemy. We ask for our rights, not gifts.'"

With an introduction like that to class warfare, the signals for Brandt's future were set. Though he was sent to an upper school, normally a preserve of the privileged classes, because of his consistently good marks, Brandt nevertheless was a rebel with a cause by the time he entered his teens.

His childhood heroes were August Bebel and Ferdinand Lassalle, the founders of the German Social Democratic party (SPD). When others joined the Boy Scouts, Brandt went into the Red Falcons, the SPD's youth movement. Before he was fifteen his teachers were sending home notes complaining that he always wore a red ribbon in his lapel. One warned his mother, "Keep your son away from politics. He's too good a student and too gifted for that." At sixteen he was chairman of Lübeck's Rosa Luxemburg Socialist Discussion Circle. Before he was seventeen he was battling Hitler Youth thugs on the streets and was charged with assault, but acquitted for lack of evidence.

In 1931 Brandt broke from the main, moderate Social Democratic party and joined the tiny, militant Socialist Workers' party. He became one of the new party's most tireless supporters.

By day he was a sales trainee with Konsum, the cooperative food store chain, and was called Frahm. At night, using the cover name Willy Brandt, he was Lübeck's most active politician. "Willy worked at politics eight days a week," recalls an old friend.

As the Nazis became stronger, much of that politicking took place underground and in early April 1933, two months after Hitler had come to power, Brandt, not yet twenty, slipped out of town, boarded a fishing boat, and headed for Norwegian exile. The next day the Gestapo came looking for him. Though he emigrated largely because he feared Nazi persecution, he was also disillusioned with the softness of the SPD's resistance to Hitler. He chose Norway because he had grown to like the country while there on a visit as a student.

In Norway Brandt was active in socialist politics and in journalism, freelanced for numerous papers in Scandinavia, wrote eight books and dozens of pamphlets. He covered the Spanish Civil War as a correspondent for Scandinavian trade union and social democratic papers, and propagandized against the Nazis in Germany.

When the Germans invaded Norway in April 1940,

95

Brandt, by that time married to a Norwegian girl named Carlota and deprived of his German citizenship by a 1938 Nazi law, went into hiding in a mountain valley. A month later he put on a Norwegian uniform so he could surrender as a prisoner of war. His only hope to avoid arrest by the Gestapo was to pose as a soldier and be released with legitimate papers from a POW camp. In 1940 he fled to Sweden where he joined other Norwegian exiles and Socialists. He sat out the war years writing.

Brandt returned to Germany in 1945 to cover the Nuremberg war crimes trials as a correspondent for a number of Scandinavian papers. When the trials were over, Norway's foreign minister, one of Brandt's best friends, asked him to stay on in Germany as press attaché—with the rank of major —at the Norwegian liaison mission to the Allied Control Council in Berlin.

Though fourteen years in exile had deprived Brandt of contact with Germany, he soon found the bonds tightening again. When he met Kurt Schumacher, the leader of the Social Democratic party in the western occupation zones, he renewed his ties with German socialism. Schumacher asked him to come to work for the SPD in its Berlin office. Brandt accepted the offer, gave up his Norwegian citizenship and his privileges as an officer and member of the occupation forces and became a German again with all the hardships which that entailed, including hunger and rationing stamps.

To his friend Halvard Lange, the Norwegian foreign minister, he wrote, "Perhaps I shall experience the greatest failure of my life here in Berlin. But if that happens, I would like to meet defeat with the feeling that I have done my duty. It would be better to be the only democrat in Germany than one of many in Norway or some other country where everyone knows what democracy is."

Brandt, whose first marriage had broken up in 1944, married Rut Hansen, another Norwegian, in 1948 and dove into Social Democratic work in Berlin.

His rise in the party organization was spectacular. He entered the first Bundestag as an observer deputy from West Berlin in 1949 at age thirty-six. By 1950 he was a member of the SPD's West Berlin executive committee. In 1951 he was elected to the West Berlin parliament. Four years later he was chosen its president and in 1957 was elected mayor of the city. In 1961 he guided West Berliners through the crisis of the Berlin Wall, then ran unsuccessfully as the SPD's candidate for the chancellorship of West Germany against Adenauer. In 1963 he was elected national chairman and leader of the Social Democratic party, running as its candidate for the top office again in 1965 against Ludwig Erhard. When Erhard's coalition government collapsed in 1966 because the Free Democrats walked out on him over a tax bill, the Christian Democrats (the SPD's political foes) looked around for a new partner, choosing Brandt. He agreed, becoming vice chancellor and foreign minister in the "large coalition" government of Chancellor Kiesinger. Two years later, in 1969, the SPD won enough votes in the national election to form the new government and Brandt became chancellor.

By any standard he is a remarkable man. He has written nearly a dozen books. Besides German he speaks three foreign languages, including English, with near-native fluency. He is as versatile a debater on the floor of parliament as he is on the campaign trail. He is young enough in spirit to remember the mistakes of his own youth, old enough to understand that young people will keep making them.

In 1966 when he decided to help the Christian Democrats by forming a coalition government with them, thousands of

Social Democrats, including his own teenaged sons, Peter and Lars, went into the streets to demonstrate against him.

As a friend of the family told me at the time, "At the present, Peter's and Lars' political views are somewhere in limbo between Walter Ulbricht's and Mao Tse-tung's." But Brandt himself merely shrugged. After seeing Peter on TV with an anti-Brandt poster, he said, "I disagree with the boys, but I respect their views. There was a time when I, too, didn't fit into any kind of pants. Short ones were too small for me and long ones too big. You have to let young people rebel in this age. Otherwise they'll never come to rest."

Within a few weeks after taking office as chancellor in October 1969, this unusual man unveiled a program for improving relations with the Soviet Union, the other Communist countries of Eastern Europe, and East Germany.

Brandt's *Ostpolitik*, as this "eastern policy " which subsequently won him the Nobel Peace Prize was called, rested on the principle that postwar developments had created an irreversible situation in Europe and that West Germany would have to live with it. Brandt was less interested in who was responsible for which past mistakes than in charting a course for the future.

His policy called for winning the trust and confidence of the Soviet Union, which remained highly suspicious of West Germany's growing economic and military power. This required assuring Moscow, through treaties, that Bonn's intentions were entirely peaceful and that it had no claims on the USSR's East European allies and dependencies, particularly East Germany, Czechoslovakia, and Poland.

Brandt also wanted to offer the hand of reconciliation to Poland, the first country the Nazis had invaded in 1939. This entailed recognition of Poland's western border along the Oder and Neisse Rivers and its claims to the provinces

Willy Brandt

of Pomerania, Silesia, and part of East Prussia. Although Churchill and Roosevelt had more or less granted these areas to Poland in 1945, the new borders had never been fixed in any treaty with a non-Communist country. All West German administrations preceding Brandt had claimed the territories, arguing that their final disposition should await a peace conference. Brandt abandoned the claim.

Finally Brandt's new policy called for recognizing the legal existence of the GDR. To make this acceptable to West Germans, he demanded and obtained guarantees for the security of West Berlin and for access to and from the city. The treaty worked out in this connection between the United States, Russia, Britain, France, East Germany, and West Germany in 1971 is the first real guarantee of safety that West Berlin has had since the 1948 blockade.

The success of Brandt's foreign policy was nothing short of sensational. Even more sensational was the widespread support it won among the West German voters. When he became chancellor in 1969 his margin in parliament had been slim. In three years it eroded, leaving him finally with a parliamentary standoff of 248 to 248 votes. In November 1972, to break the stalemate, he called a new election in which his Social Democratic and the Free Democratic parties ended up with a majority of 48 seats in the Bundestag.

However, in the spring of 1974 a scandal precipitated Brandt's unexpected resignation. An East German spy, Günter Guillaume, had been infiltrated into Brandt's office in early 1970. When Guillaume was arrested four years later and the scope of the intrigue became evident, Brandt abruptly resigned.

Ironically, when Honecker became head of the SED in 1971, he had retained for himself the supervision of security and intelligence operations. He therefore exercised operational control over Guillaume and must share at least indirectly much of the responsibility for Brandt's fall.

There were other reasons for Brandt's decision. Ever since the smashing November 1972 victory, the coalition had been squabbling among itself. Moreover, West Germany had been facing mounting domestic troubles, in particular an inflationary economy, which Brandt, more interested in foreign than internal matters, seemed incapable of dealing with effectively. In Brandt's discouraged state of mind, the discovery of Honecker's spy was the final blow.

Since the coalition had a solid majority in parliament until 1976, a new election was not necessary under West Germany's system. Another Social Democrat, Helmut Schmidt, became the new chancellor, while Brandt agreed to continue temporarily as leader of the SPD.

Born in 1918 in Hamburg, Schmidt is a pragmatic former minister of defense and finance minister, tougher but less visionary than Brandt. It was obvious when he took office in May 1974 that his governmental style would be different. He let it be known immediately that relations between the two Germanys would be strained for a while because of the spy affair, but that the daring experiment of peaceful coexistence between the two Germanys would continue.

Two Germans, Adenauer and Ulbricht, different in background and politics yet alike in manners and character, presided over Germany's division into two countries.

Two other Germans, Honecker and Brandt, similar in youthful experience yet different in character and politics, led the Germanys to political maturity and launched the first attempts at peaceful coexistence.

As Schmidt and other new leaders come to power, only the future will tell whether the attempts will succeed.

5
Two Kinds of Democracy?

"We have taken democracy from the coat rack of history and put it on like a cloak," a senior West German government official once told me. "The entire world wonders what is underneath. I am not sure myself, but I do believe that clothes tend to change a man. By wearing the cloak of democracy long enough the personality of Germany itself may change."

Each of the two Germanys has taken a mantle of democracy from the hanger and claims to be democratic. Both have constitutions which guarantee their citizens the same basic human rights: freedom of speech, the press, religion, assembly, freedom from want and fear, equality before the law, the right to vote at age eighteen, and the presumption of innocence before being proven guilty.

Nevertheless each Germany accuses the other of being undemocratic and unfree.

To West Germany the GDR is a totalitarian state because it has no really free elections, no real choice of political parties or candidates, a centrally controlled press with censorship, and a vast secret police organization which keeps a sharp eye on all citizens. It has walled its people up and refuses to let them leave the country. The GDR's constitution, according to West Germany, is not worth the paper it is printed on because its principles are violated by the regime every day.

To East Germany the FRG is an undemocratic state because it is capitalist. According to East German theory, there can be no real democracy in a country in which the means of production are owned by the few who then can use the power of their money to exploit and control the lives of the many. A choice of political parties and candidates, says East Germany, means nothing as long as all are the pawns of big business. There can be no real freedom of the press, according to East Germany, as long as the papers and publishing houses are owned by a handful of rich men who can manipulate the opinions of the masses. Nor, the GDR contends, can there be real equality before the law as long as the rich and powerful can influence the government, control the courts, and buy the best lawyers.

West Germany argues that virtually all power in the GDR is vested in the Socialist Unity party (SED) and that this party exercises monopolistic control over the entire society. East Germany contends that all power in the FRG is in the hands of the monopolists of industry.

The positions are obviously pretty far apart. And they are not likely to move closer as long as both sides fail to agree on a definition of democracy. Even if it were a proper forum, there would be no space in this book to resolve the argument. Let us just say there is some merit to the views of both sides, although in the long run it is not theory but practice that proves the value of a political system. And there is no doubt in my mind that practice has proven West Germany's infinitely more democratic than the GDR's.

West Germany's constitution, or Basic Law as it is called, was drafted in the ivory tower atmosphere of Bonn by sixty-five old men whose only previous experience with democracy was during the brief period of the Weimar Republic. The document they came up with in May 1949 reflected the views and opinions of the American, British, and French military governors who had to approve it and an earnest desire to avoid the mistakes made at Weimar.

It is based on the principle of federalism, much like the Constitution of the United States. A great deal of power is vested in the ten states, or *Länder,* that comprise the Federal Republic: Bavaria, Baden-Württemberg, Hesse, Rhineland-Palatinate, North Rhine-Westphalia, Lower Saxony, Saarland, Schleswig-Holstein, and the two city-states of Hamburg and Bremen. West Berlin has a special status. According to a plan now under consideration, the number of states may be reduced to six or five by combining some of the smaller ones or incorporating them into the larger Länder.

Each *Land* has its own legislature whose representatives are elected every four years by the people. Each legislature, called a *Landtag,* elects a minister-president who chooses his cabinet members from among the legislators.

Although the minister-presidents serve a function comparable to that of the governors of American states, they are more powerful than governors because they also represent their states in the *Bundesrat,* the upper house, or senate, of the federal parliament. The Bundesrat is not as important or as powerful as the United States Senate, but it plays a similar role. It must approve all legislation passed by the lower house, the *Bundestag*. Unlike the United States Senate, however, members of the Bundesrat are not elected directly by the people. They are appointed by the state legislatures. Nor does each Land have an equal voice. The size of the Land delegation to the Bundesrat varies from three to five members and depends on the Land's population.

There were two reasons for federalization.

Traditionally some states, like the Rhineland, had always been separatist and others, like Bavaria and Württemberg, which once had been independent kingdoms, insisted on strong local powers. They all wanted a system of guarantees that would prevent any one state from again dominating the others as Prussia had done.

Secondly Hitler had consolidated his power by completely destroying local government. He had centralized the police as well as the educational system and the instruments of information, such as radio stations, which then became tools of Nazi propaganda. The Bonn convention wanted to prevent that from happening again.

Even more important than federalization, however, was a system of guarantees for stable government. The authors of the Bonn constitution remembered with horror the Weimar Republic in which shifting alliances between dozens of little political parties and the weakness of the chancellorship had resulted in a succession of governments, some of which lasted only a few days. It was this weakness that made the rise of a strong man like Hitler possible.

The trouble with the Weimar Republic had been that the president, elected directly by the people, was too strong; that parliament had too many small parties in it; that the

West Germany's Bundestag in session

chancellor, elected by parliament, had too few powers.

Under the Bonn constitution the federal president is strictly a figurehead. Instead of being elected by the people, he is chosen by a Federal Assembly, made up of all the members of the Bundestag and an equivalent number of representatives from the Land parliaments. He serves a five-year term and may be re-elected once.

During the Weimar Republic there were at one time as many as thirty-six political parties running against each other, and for each 30,000 popular votes that a party received, it was entitled to one seat in the Reichstag. Many of these parties were extremist and splinter groups that had no interest in making democracy work but in destroying it. They made governing the country next to impossible. The framers of the Bonn constitution created several obstacles against a repetition of this, the most important being the "5 per cent barrier." To be represented at all, unless it wins a direct mandate in a district, a party must get at least 5 per cent of the total number of votes cast in the country.

Finally the position of the chancellor was strengthened. As the nation's chief executive, he is responsible only to the Bundestag and enjoys powers somewhere between those of the US president and the British prime minister. Like the British prime minister, he is elected by a majority of all the members of the house; in practice, he is the leader of the largest, most popular party or the party that obtains the backing of more than half the Bundestag members. He names his own cabinet ministers, the choice not being subject to further approval by the Bundestag. They are responsible to the chancellor, the chancellor to parliament.

Theoretically, the chancellor and his government could be tossed out of office, like the prime ministers of other parliamentary systems, through a "vote of no confidence." But under the Bonn constitution it requires a "constructive vote of no confidence," which means that a majority of all the members of the Bundestag must choose a successor and ask the federal president to dismiss the incumbent chancellor before a new one can take office. In practice, drumming up a majority for a move like that is next to impossible.

The result of these safeguards has been that West Germany has had a very stable government since 1949. In twenty-five years there have been only five chancellors, compared to the dozen during the fourteen years of the Weimar Republic. The number of political parties represented in the Bundestag and the Land legislatures has dwindled steadily to the point where the Federal Republic now has a very solid three-party system: the Social Democrats (SPD) and the Christian Democrats (CDU/CSU), who between them average nearly 90 per cent of the votes cast, and the Free Democrats (FDP), who account for about 10 per cent. In a quarter century there has been only one real government crisis. That was in 1972 when so many SPD and FDP Bundestag deputies bolted party ranks and joined the CDU opposition because of Willy Brandt's foreign policy, that the SPD-FDP coalition government lost its majority in the house, which caused the stalemate at 248 to 248 votes. Brandt decided to dissolve parliament and called for a new election, in which his Social Democrats and the coalition Free Democrats won a majority. So when Brandt resigned in May 1974, another Social Democrat, Helmut Schmidt, was simply nominated as chancellor and elected in the Bundestag.

This by any standard is a remarkable record. Not even the most optimistic observer would have predicted such stability fifteen or twenty years ago. It is a record of which West Germany's European neighbors with much longer traditions of democracy can be envious.

Two Kinds of Democracy?

"In the first years," Erich Mende, a member of the Bundestag and former vice-chancellor under both Adenauer and Erhard, once told me, "the idea of parliamentary democracy was not very popular. There was a lot of criticism of the officials in Bonn. There was no real understanding of government by discussion. But today democracy and parliamentary procedures are deeply rooted, above all among the young people."

Indeed in the early 1950s when the infant Federal Republic was taking its first hesitant steps, most of its citizens did not take it very seriously and had no sense of deep loyalty to it. Nobody could forget the chaos of the Weimar Republic and among many people, raised in a country which had never really experienced a successful democracy, there was still a secret yearning for a strong man like Hitler, despite the misery he had brought his people and the world.

In those days buses filled with gawking rubbernecks would cruise at snail's pace past the ugly, concrete former teachers' college that houses the Bonn parliament. Excursion boats on the Rhine only a few yards away would draw close to the bank. And the passengers on the buses and boats would taunt parliament with a popular carnival song:

> *Who is going to pay for this,*
> *Who ordered this for us?*
> *Who has enough moola,*
> *Who has this much dough?*

Nowadays the boats and buses disgorge their passengers into the parliament building to sit attentively in the visitors' galleries and listen to the debates. The song is no longer heard and Germans take their parliament seriously. So seriously in fact that in April 1972, when Rainer Barzel, the leader of the CDU/CSU in the Bundestag, tried to oust

Brandt's government with a "constructive vote of no confidence," hundreds of thousands of West Germans took to the streets to demonstrate. In its brief experience with democracy the Federal Republic had witnessed countless spontaneous mass demonstrations. Virtually all had been against the government. But these were on its behalf.

During the first Bundestag election in 1949 about 78 per cent of the eligible voters went to the polls. Nowadays the average is close to 90 per cent. Millions of Germans are members of the large political parties or belong to political action groups which play important roles on the local as well as the federal scene.

The big question being asked abroad in all those years was whether Germany was immune to a Nazi revival. There was a time when this did not seem at all certain. In the late 1960s for example, the National Democratic party with an ultraright-wing, neo-Nazi platform became very strong. One by one it began capturing seats in the Land parliaments. But then it vanished from the scene almost as suddenly as it had appeared. In April 1972 the party decided not to run in the state election in Baden-Württemberg where four years previously it had won 9.8 per cent of the votes. Thus it lost its last remaining seats in any state legislature in Germany. The party is now dead.

The real test of Bonn's democracy, however, was not how it would weather the storm of a neo-Nazi revival but how it would ride out the first real transition of power from a Christian Democratic to a Social Democratic government.

To understand the significance of that transition we must go back to Germany's defeat, the Kaiser's abdication, and the creation of the Weimar Republic under President Friedrich Ebert in 1918. Those events were for many decades regarded as a sellout of the idea of a strong Reich. The loss of World War I had been blamed on "treason on the home front." Because Ebert, the first president in 1918, had been a Social Democrat, his party for many subsequent decades, right through the Hitler era and into the period after World War II, labored under the stigma of disloyalty.

Konrad Adenauer had himself capitalized on that innate public distrust. In the turbulent election campaigns of the 1950s he likened his CDU to Christian good, the SDP to Bolshevik evil. He portrayed the Social Democrats as the "red menace." In the 1961 campaign he denigrated himself and the new democracy he purported to represent by referring to Brandt's illegitimate birth and implying that Brandt had been less than patriotic in fleeing to Scandinavia when Hitler came to power. Adenauer equated opposition to himself in parliament with opposition to the state.

In the emotion-charged atmosphere of those Cold War days when the SPD opposed NATO and West German rearmament, Adenauer's tactics may have been smart politics, but they did a disservice to German democracy.

When Brandt finally won in 1969, the traditional roles in Bonn changed. Opposition at last became respectable in the German mind, for the CDU, which had been the government for twenty years, was suddenly "the opposition." As a result the Bundestag became a forum for meaningful parliamentary debate.

Brandt's victory was an orderly transition of power—the first of its kind that Germany had had since 1918. Upon taking office he said, "In the past, many in this country feared that Germany's second democracy would go the way of the first. I have never believed this. I believe it even less today. We are not at the end of our democracy, we are at its beginning."

Events following Brandt's own resignation in 1974 vindicated his faith. The transfer of power to his successor, Helmut Schmidt, was carried out with scarcely a ripple.

Power in West Germany rests with parliament and the chancellor. In the GDR, despite a fine-sounding constitution and all manner of guarantees and safeguards, power is vested in the ruling Socialist Unity Party, more specifically, in its Central Committee and its Politburo. The most powerful man in the country is the first secretary of the Central Committee. That used to be Walter Ulbricht. Now it is Erich Honecker.

That party has had a unique history. It is a union between Communists and Social Democrats, the two political groups that evolved out of the split between prowar and antiwar socialists during World War I. After 1918 they had become separate parties and the bitterest political enemies, though they continued to have many ideas in common. Between them they controlled almost half the votes in the Weimar Republic, but they were so opposed to each other they they could never join forces to fight the chaos and the rising menace of Nazism.

When Hitler came to power in 1933, he outlawed both parties. Many members of both were placed in concentration camps. Many others emigrated. Some went underground and somehow managed to survive the Nazi tyranny. In 1945, when the Social Democrats and Communists resurfaced, there were strong forces for reuniting the two parties. The advocates of union—those Communists who had been in the camps and those Social Democrats living in the Soviet occupation zone who had fought a common battle against the Nazis, had endured mutual suffering in Gestapo jails, and had glossed over the cracks of disagreement—felt strongly that Hitler's road to power had been paved largely by the split in the German working-class movement.

That view was not shared by the Social Democrats in the western zones nor by the Communist party (KPD) leadership, made up primarily of men who had fled to Moscow and had spent the Hitler years there.

In May and June 1945 Otto Grotewohl and Max Fechner, the leaders of the Soviet Zone Social Democrats (SPD), met numerous times with Walter Ulbricht, the German Communist chief, and urged him to form a united party. "The time is not ripe," insisted Ulbricht, rejecting the proposal.

Ulbricht feared that the Communists were not yet strong enough to dominate a unified party. He needed time to consolidate control over the KPD. Many of its members who had remained in Germany were not yet ready to take orders from Stalin-trained party bosses like Ulbricht who had been away in comfortable Moscow exile.

But Ulbricht changed his mind as he saw the SPD getting more popular while the Communists began losing ground in local elections. By the end of 1945 it was Ulbricht who was pushing union while opposition from Social Democrats in the western zones, under the leadership of Dr. Kurt Schumacher, mounted.

Ulbricht began encouraging "spontaneous amalgamation" on the local and state level, often under the bumbling pressure of Soviet military government chiefs.

On April 21, 1946, the union of Soviet zone Communists and Socialists was completed, and the new party, the Socialist Unity party (SED), which has ruled East Germany ever since, was born. In a ceremony in an East Berlin theater, Wilhelm Pieck, the nominal head of the KPD, and Grotewohl approached each other from opposing wings on the stage, met in the center, and just the way the party's emblem depicts it, shook hands. "Wilhelm Pieck," said Grotewohl, "came from the left. I came from the right. We both came to meet in the middle."

Grotewohl was soon to learn that Pieck had not met him halfway. In fact, Grotewohl had become junior partner in a party rushing headlong on the Stalinist path. What had originated as a brotherhood of equals soon became an instrument of Soviet policy in which many loyal Communists had little and the Socialists far less to say.

The Social Democrats, who had come halfway to build a unified party with the Communists, were suppressed, silenced, sidelined, and subjugated until all that remained of social democracy in East Germany was memories.

The other political parties originally allowed to form in the Soviet zone in 1945, the Christian Democrats (CDU) and the Liberal Democrats (LDPD), fared no better, though they still exist in name. They had posed no real ballot box threat to the new Socialist Unity party. In fact, during the last honest elections in East Germany in 1946, the Socialist Unity party did well. It won 53 per cent of the vote in Saxony's September municipal and county elections and 60 per cent in those held in Brandenburg and Mecklenburg. But Ulbricht was not satisfied with majorities. He wanted total control.

Backed by the Russians, he began the systematic liquidation of western-style democracy. Soviet military government officials caused the non-Communist parties as much trouble as possible. Their members were barred from civil service jobs, responsible positions, and from attending colleges or university. Many Christian Democrat and Liberal Democrat politicians fled to West Berlin and West Germany. Their defections left vacuums that the Soviets filled with their own hand-picked puppets.

114

In 1948 the Soviets created two additional political groups: the National Democrats (not to be confused with the similarly named right-wing party in West Germany) and the Democratic Farmers' party (DBD). Their purpose was to give East Germany an appearance of democracy and popular will, though both these parties are nothing but artificial satellites of the SED.

All four of these non-Communist parties, that is, the Christian, Liberal, and National Democrats, and the Socialist Unity party and several so-called mass organizations such as the Free German Youth group, the Free German Trade Union Federation, and the Federation of Democratic German Women comprise the "National Front," which fields a single ticket of candidates for elections to the *Volksammer*, East Germany's parliament.

But you cannot call these parties democratic and they cannot be compared with political parties in the western sense. Although there are currents of different opinion among the 1.7 million members of the Socialist Unity Party, the dues-paying, card-holding 300,000 who belong to the four non-Communist parties are nothing more than a false front opposition.

Their leaders of course try to justify their existence. Thus a Liberal Democratic party spokesman once told me, "We represent the interests of little businessmen, farmers, and professionals, who although they approve of communism, do not want to join the Socialist Unity party. No, we do not have a political program of our own. We support the Socialist Unity party's." Why then, I asked him, have a separate political party at all? "Oh," he replied with exasperation, "you just don't understand."

There was a time when these non-Communist parties did represent some opposition. But over the years their leaders have been worn down by pressure, blackmail, and the lures of privilege. They made their peace with Ulbricht who rewarded them for playing his game. They have become members of the East German elite, serve in the Volkskammer, and have second-rate government posts. They are non-Communist only in name.

The regime measures its popularity not so much by the number of votes it receives but by the percentage of the election turnout. It is an obligation to vote. Even the crippled are carted to the polls. To refuse to vote is like disapproving of motherhood and God. As a result, participation is usually 98.8 per cent.

The obligation to vote is as binding as the duty to work and produce for the state; and the propaganda spurring East Germans to do one or the other sounds essentially the same. Signs on factory buildings announce that the workers have improved their efficiency as "our contribution to the election." It is not unusual to see collective farms promising to breed more and fatter pigs "in honor of the people's election."

For nearly twenty years these elections were always "ivory pure" travesties of democracy. There was only one ticket, the National Front's, on which the number of candidates was equal to the number of jobs to be filled. Voters faced three choices: to approve the whole ticket, to reject it, or to boycott the election. The latter two required nearly superhuman courage.

Those who approved the ticket voted in full public view. Those who opposed it could demand to go to a voting booth, usually located in a far corner of the room, but the path to it always led past the disapproving glances of election officials, many of whom served the secret police. Consequently 99.9 per cent of the voters usually approved the ticket.

A mass rally in East Germany on the eve of a referendum

In 1967 the electoral system was changed slightly. A system of "reserve candidates" was introduced. These exceed the number of posts to be filled by 20 per cent. All candidates are still on the same National Front ticket, but voters can choose them individually. If one of the regular candidates receives less than 50 per cent of the votes cast, he is disqualified and the reserve candidate with the highest number of votes moves up a slot to take his place. This is not what we would call an election, but it is at least a selection process.

Some East Germans claim that they exercise far more influence over their elected representatives than is generally assumed by western observers.

"We may not have a choice of parties," an East German steel worker once told me, "but we know who the candidates are and they get a careful screening from everyone before they are even listed on the ballot. They have to answer questions in factory and neighborhood meetings and the cross-examination is often quite stiff.

"In West Germany," he added, "what choice does the voter really have? He can pick between parties, but he has little influence on the candidates they have proposed. These are nominated by a party machine over which the members, not to mention the vast majority of voters, have no control. Ninety-nine times out of a hundred the voter won't know anything about the candidates when the time comes to vote. The West jokes about our single ticket and the National Front, but plenty of people here prefer knowing all about the candidate before the election than having to choose between names which mean nothing and being represented by men and women over whom they have no leverage."

Despite liberalization of the electoral system, the GDR remains essentially a totalitarian regime in which democratic institutions play a superficial and artificial role.

The Volkskammer is basically a rubber-stamp parliament. It meets only twice a year for a few days and generally approves all legislation unanimously and without debate. In fact, the first and only time there were dissenting votes in it was in 1972 when it passed a law legalizing abortion in the GDR.

East Germany's highest organ is the State Council, or *Staatsrat*, a twenty-six-man "collective presidency," of which Ulbricht was chairman until his death in 1973. Established in 1960, it was tailor-made from the outset to satisfy the ambitions of Ulbricht, who until then had merely been a deputy prime minister. Its chairman since October 1973 has been Willi Stoph.

The executive branch is the Council of Ministers, or *Ministerrat*, the closest thing the GDR has to a Western-style cabinet. Its forty-three members are appointed by the Volkskammer. Horst Sindermann, its chairman, is the head of the East German government and fills a role similar to that of a prime minister or West Germany's chancellor. In addition to the chairman, there are twelve deputy chairmen and thirty regular members who are called ministers.

Since nearly all industries are owned by the state, they are run by the government. As a result, the Council of Ministers is responsible not only for typical government functions such as defense, foreign affairs, justice, health, education, and welfare but also for those activities which in a non-Communist country would fall to big business and private enterprise. Thus besides standard government departments there are also ministers of construction, electronics, heavy machinery, chemicals, light industry, and so on.

Despite its seeming importance the Council of Ministers is primarily an administrative body, part of a chain of command in which the real orders and decisions come from somewhere else: the Politburo and the Secretariat of the Socialist Unity party.

The Politburo (Political Bureau of the Central Committee of the Socialist Unity Party) is made up of six members. They determine East Germany's foreign policy, decide the pace of the economy, set the ideological course, and exercise control over the National People's Army, the People's Police, and the State Security Service. They meet at least once a week, much like a Western cabinet, and reach their decisions in the way a jury arrives at a verdict—by discussion until there is agreement.

Even more important and powerful than the Politburo is the Central Committee's Secretariat, headed by Honecker, the first secretary. Besides him there are ten other secretaries, most of them members of the Politburo as well, each of whom is responsible for a specific SED party department such as agriculture, foreign trade, the economy, propaganda, security, culture, and education.

According to East German doctrine, the Socialist Unity party "plays the leading role in society." That means that the party's Politburo and Secretariat are the GDR's real but invisible government.

In theory both the Politburo and the Secretariat are responsible to and take their orders from the party's Central Committee, a body of 135 voting and 54 nonvoting members who are chosen by the party conventions held every four years. The Central Committee meets at least once every six months and, nominally, it is the party's legislature. All the party secretaries, Politburo members, leading ministers and government officials, local and regional party bosses, educators, writers, and the managers and directors of the biggest state-owned industrial plants and collective farms belong to it. In practice, however, the Central Committee is as much a rubber-stamp parliament as the Volkskammer. The SED, like other Communist parties, practices what Lenin called "democratic centralism." Under democratic centralism the party's leadership is elected from below, but once in power it has complete authority, and its decisions and policies are binding on the lower echelons and the rank and file members. This means that the top leaders decide who will be a delegate to the party convention and who is elected to the Central Committee.

Like West Germany, the GDR also has a constitution and it promises East Germans the same basic human rights that Americans take for granted. But the promises are frequently broken.

On paper, at least, East Germans are allowed to criticize their government and the state, but when they do so they run the risk of being indicted for antistate propaganda and agitation. There are an estimated 8,000 political prisoners serving terms for such crimes. Some of them are teenagers and students who in August 1968 demonstrated against the Soviet and East German invasion of Czechoslovakia.

Freedom of the press is guaranteed, but since all newspapers and magazines are published either by the government, the SED, or the puppet non-Communist parties, they only express the official view. All books are published by party and government publishing houses and undergo strict censorship. Authors who write too critically or deviate from the official political line, just do not get into print. It is illegal to start one's own newspaper or magazine or to publish one's own book. It is also illegal to import magazines, newspapers, and books from the western capitalist countries unless these have been approved by the censor's office. Generally only technical journals get approval. Reading material brought in by western visitors is usually confiscated at the borders.

Even playing "capitalist" pop music is illegal. In 1973 disc jockeys in East German discotheques and dance clubs were warned that they would be fined 1,000 marks for playing records from western countries. The GDR considers such records, which sell for fantastic prices on the black market, "anti-Communist."

The GDR, in other words, is a totalitarian state. But even so, there is more control from below and a greater measure of democratic influence than is generally assumed in the West.

It is important to remember that the Socialist Unity party has 1.7 million dues-paying and card-holding members. This represents about 15 per cent of the adult population of the country. The party may not be the world's most democratic one, but membership is not only voluntary it is considered a privilege, and those who belong to it must believe that it has something to offer.

How would that party and the regime fare if East Germany suddenly had completely free elections? No one can say for sure, of course, but in the years that I have traveled in the GDR and studied its political system I have gained the impression that the SED would come close to 50 per cent of the vote. That is as good or better as the Social Democrats and the Christian Democrats have done in West Germany. Unfortunately, however, I doubt whether the leaders of the SED will ever have the courage to put their party and their system to a real test vote.

6
Man-Made Miracles

When the bombs stopped dropping, the guns stopped shooting, and the nightmare of the Third Reich came to an end in May 1945, the pressure gauges of the German economy pointed to zero. Germany was like a cadaver—without circulation. Flattened by years of bombardment, ravaged by battle, bled of its youth and sense of purpose, there seemed no prospect of recovery.

Some 6 to 7 million Germans, both soldiers and civilians, had been killed, and an estimated 12 million German men were in prisoner of war camps.

About 20 per cent of all dwelling units had been totally destroyed, with destruction in large urban areas such as Berlin, Hamburg, Dresden, Cologne, and Munich ranging between 50 and 75 per cent.

The transportation and communications networks were in a state of chaos. Nearly all road and rail bridges had been bombed. More than half the railway freight cars were lost.

Although bombing and war action had destroyed only 20 per cent of Germany's total industrial capacity, the western allies, particularly the French, dismantled and demolished about 8 per cent of what remained in their zones; the Russians carted off more than 45 per cent in theirs.

The first postwar winter was an especially severe one with critical shortages of food, fuel, and clothing. The second winter, 1946 to 1947, was even worse and had been preceded by an unusually poor harvest.

In towns and cities the average daily food intake often dropped to as low as 800 calories (nutrition experts say 2,000 is the minimum requirement). Disease and hunger were rampant. To keep alive, city dwellers scavenged the countryside in search of food, offering farmers clothing, bedding, chinaware, furniture, and family heirlooms—whatever might be considered of value—in exchange for a few pounds of flour or potatoes.

Other supplies were also desperately short. Coal and wood for heating were rationed. There was enough cloth to provide only every fortieth man with one suit a year, every tenth with a shirt. Only one in seven could be provided with a plate, one in five with a toothbrush, and one in 150 with a washbowl. Wood was so scarce that only every third body could be provided with a coffin in which to be buried.

The first three years were years of total despair. A black market in scarce commodities flourished everywhere. Children with no schools to attend became black-market operators. To steal was no longer regarded as a moral crime. In fact parents encouraged their children to steal—coal from railway yards, potatoes from farmers' hoards—anything to

Dresden, East Germany, after World War II

keep alive. Instead of money, cigarettes became the unit of currency and for one or two a man could buy a woman for a night.

A quarter century later the two Germanys that have arisen from this chaos are the envy of their less affluent neighbors and allies. West Germany ranks along with the US, the USSR, and Japan, among the big four of the world's industrial and trading nations; East Germany has a solid place among the top ten. Both are hard-driving export countries whose products are in demand around the world for their precision, reliability, excellent workmanship, and sensible design. Both have experienced economic miracles unmatched by any other country with the exception perhaps of Japan, another defeated World War II power. Their success has been so spectacular that it has given rise to the comment that "it paid to lose the war."

In late 1947 and early 1948 West German industrial production was only about half of what it had been before the war. But by 1950 industrial output had already exceeded prewar figures and the West Germans were enjoying a better life than they had had in 1938, the last full peacetime year.

East Germany, with only a fourth of the population and the territory and a fraction of the industrial capacity and resources, was producing more in 1964 than the entire German Reich, including the territories ceded to Poland, had produced in 1938.

And both Germanys continue to grow and to expand—at a rate of about 4.5 per cent annually.

Their cities have been rebuilt. West Germany has built some 10 million new homes and apartments, East Germany more than 1 million. Both Germanys are now consumer-oriented societies, just as both are welfare states, having continued the social security programs started by Bismarck in the nineteenth century.

Except for brief dips in the economy such as that caused by the world-wide energy shortage in late 1973 and early 1974, both Germanys have enjoyed virtually full employment.

West Germany, which absorbed some eight million refugees and expellees from the Soviet zone and the Polish-occupied territories of the Reich, had to hire 2.5 million foreigners, primarily from Turkey, Yugoslavia, Italy, Greece, and Spain to keep the wheels of industry, trade, and services rolling. East Germany not only lost millions of people as a result of the refugee movement, but lost the very ones who were most productive. It has a population which is critically overage and it does not expect an increase in its native labor force until 1980. Women account for 46 per cent of the country's gainfully employed, which means in practice that more than three out of four adult women work outside the home. On top of that the GDR has recruited 30,000 "guest workers" from Hungary and an estimated 15,000 from neighboring Poland.

How did the two Germanys do it and how do they compare?

The turning point for West Germany was the spring of 1948 when it began receiving the first of some $3.8 billion in loans and grants from America as part of the Marshall Plan, the US program to help war-ravaged Europe back to its feet so that it would be economically independent.

The start of the Marshall Plan was followed by the currency reform in June 1948. This measure, which was so opposed by the Soviets and led to the Berlin Blockade, put an end to the black market almost overnight by wiping out all excess money. To finance the war, the Nazis had printed money wildly with nothing backing it up, and by 1948 there were eleven times more Reichsmarks in circulation than there had been in 1938. The money of course was practically worthless and bought nothing. No one wanted it. Although industry had resumed production, neither factories nor wholesalers nor retailers wanted to sell goods for money in which they had no confidence. Under the currency reform the Reichsmark was abolished and replaced by the Deutsche mark at a rate of 10 Reichsmarks for one Deutsche mark. No sooner had the new money been distributed than goods reappeared from their hiding places in warehouses and underneath shop counters. And as the goods reappeared on the market, people were willing to work to buy them. The new mark became the barometer of West Germany's recovery. When it was first introduced it took only 24 American cents to buy one. Today the DM is one of the world's strongest currencies and at one point in 1973 cost about 41 US cents.

Finally there was the economic system itself, introduced by Professor Ludwig Erhard, the first economics minister. Erhard, who succeeded Adenauer as chancellor in 1963, was called "Mr. D-mark." A pink-faced, dumpling-shaped man whose ever-present cigar became the symbol of West Germany's success, Erhard inaugurated the "social market economy." Basically this is a free-enterprise system in which the forces of supply and demand are allowed to operate freely. For Germany it represented a sharp departure from tradition as its economy had been tightly controlled under Hitler and even at times during the Weimar Republic. It was not, however, a free-for-all type of system. It placed strong controls on monopoly-building and broke up some of the biggest ones. It acknowledged the responsibility of the state in maintaining order by regulating credit, foreign trade, and preserving harmony between labor and management.

Today West Germany is the biggest industrial power in Europe and the richest member of the Common Market. In the non-Communist world it runs neck and neck with Japan and right behind the United States itself. It produces more steel, chemicals, automobiles, trucks, electrical and electronic goods, textiles, and plastics than Great Britain, France, or Italy. Each year it exports about $5 billion more than it imports. This not only makes West Germany the most successful trading nation in the world but through its exports it has amassed the world's largest reserve of foreign currency, especially dollars.

Who owns and controls all this wealth? That question touches on one of the most controversial issues in West Germany today.

Some of West Germany's industry is—and has always been—owned by American corporations. For example, the Opel automobile plant, Germany's third largest, has been a subsidiary of General Motors Corporation since the 1920s. Oddly, although it was making trucks for the *Wehrmacht* during World War II, it suffered almost no damage during bombing raids. The German Ford plant in Cologne, Germany's fourth largest automobile manufacturer, is wholly owned by the American Ford Motor Company. Other big American operators on the German market, either with subsidiaries or as owners of previously German companies are Exxon, International Business Machines, Sperry Rand, International Telephone and Telegraph, Mobil Oil Company, Texaco, Goodyear Tire and Rubber Company, Firestone Tire and Rubber Company, Boeing, General Foods, Swift

On the wharf in Bremen, new Volkswagens stand ready for export.

and Company, Armour Company, National Dairy Products, and North American Rockwell Corporation.

American holdings in Germany represent only about 8 per cent of the total. However, American companies or US-owned subsidiaries play an especially large role in certain key fields such as automobile manufacturing, petroleum products, electronics, and data processing. This has enabled extremist political groups to make political capital out of German fears of a "Yankee take-over." The ultrarightist *Deutsche National und Soldaten Zeitung*, a rabble-rousing weekly with a large circulation, charges that America's role in the German economy "is not different from Soviet domination of East Germany."

An even touchier issue than American control, however, is the fact that Germany's wealth and its means of production are concentrated in very few hands. Although the standard of living has improved steadily and the average West German today lives better than all of his European neighbors with the exception of the Swiss and the Swedes, the gap between the affluent and the rest of society has also widened steadily since 1948. The common man has gained a degree of comfort which would have been unthinkable a quarter century ago. But the rich have gotten super rich. There are nearly 18,000 men and women whose personal fortunes exceed DM 1 million. The thirty-four richest have annual incomes of more than DM 10 million per year. Five per cent of the population owns about 67 per cent of the wealth, the remaining 95 per cent own only 33 per cent. The biggest names—Flick, Thyssen, Siemens, Bosch, Quandt, and Oetker—have combined resources four times greater than those of the 13 million people in their employ.

Unlike other European countries that have moved toward government ownership of some of the biggest enterprises,

West Germany, even under the Social Democratic Party, has opted for private control. While other countries were nationalizing, West Germany was denationalizing. Its biggest corporation, the Volkswagen Company, started out in 1937 as a government-owned enterprise. In 1963 it was made private and stock was sold to the general public. Big banks own much of it today.

There are now strong pressures in West Germany to reverse this process, that is, to place more of industry under some effective form of public control, to give labor a greater voice in the running of industry, and to assure a more equal distribution of wealth. Early in 1974 a bill was introduced in the Bundestag to give representatives of labor an equal voice on the supervisory boards of large corporations employing 2,000 or more people. Another bill makes a kind of profit-sharing system mandatory for most companies. Although both measures are certain to become law, the issue itself is sure to remain one of the biggest in domestic West German politics for years to come.

But one thing is certain. Even without a spread of authority and wealth, the average West German today enjoys one of the highest standards of living in the world, a standard of living he would not have dreamed of in those dark days after the end of World War II.

West Germany began with nothing. But as a young East German executive once said to me, "East Germany began with less than nothing."

Geographically, in terms of natural resources, and industrial, transportation, and communications capacity, the Soviet zone was at a tremendous disadvantage.

First of all, it had no major port, Stettin having been ceded to Poland, Lübeck being part of the British zones. The only significant rivers are the Oder and the Elbe, but the GDR has no control of the estuaries of either. The Oder, which forms the frontier with Poland for most of its navigable course, empties into the Baltic Sea in what is now Polish territory. The Elbe, which rises in Czechoslovakia, crosses East Germany from Dresden to Magdeburg but then enters West German territory and flows into the North Sea at Hamburg.

Prewar Germany's highway and railway system, including Hitler's vaunted autobahn network, ran on an east–west axis. To this day, for example, there is only one main railway line and a narrow, winding highway to connect East Germany's manufacturing heartland with the new port of Rostock which the GDR began building on the Baltic coast in 1957. The rail line is not electrified and plans do not call for its conversion from steam until 1977. Construction of a four-lane freeway did not begin until 1971, and it will not be completed before 1980. Nor does Rostock, which now handles more than twice as much freight as San Francisco, have water connections to the south. The Warnow River, which empties into the Baltic there, is only sixty miles long. It is not navigable and it does not lead anywhere except to the flat farmlands of Mecklenburg.

To these physical disadvantages one must add the lack of raw materials. The Soviet zone had virtually no deposits of hard anthracite coal, the only ones being in the Zwickau area of Saxony where the total reserves are estimated at less than 35 million tons today, or about one third of West Germany's annual anthracite production. The supplies of iron ore, nonferrous metals, oil, and natural gas are too small to even mention. There is virtually no water power to harness. Although the GDR now produces 69 billion kilowatt hours of electric power each year, more than is produced by Holland, Belgium, Sweden, Switzerland, Norway,

Australia, or India, only 1.8 per cent of this is generated by hydroelectric stations. The vast majority—86 per cent—is produced by thermal power plants using soft brown lignite coal of which the GDR has an overabundance.

Lignite, a very inefficient energy source because of its high water and sand content and the costs of conversion, is just about the GDR's only raw materials asset. Reserves are more than 40 billion tons and the GDR is the world's largest producer of it. East Germany runs on brown coal, whose acrid smell distinguishes the GDR from West Germany the minute you step across the border. It not only provides most of the power but serves as a source for artificial high-temperature coke, gas, and liquid derivatives such as phenol, tars, motor fuel, and plastics. No matter how it is used though, it has a repulsive odor, is wasteful, and unprofitable.

In addition to lignite, East Germany's only other natural resources are substantial deposits of potash and mineral salts, limestone, and raw materials for the glass, optical, ceramic, and chemical industries.

But East Germany was handicapped in more ways than just the lack of resources and geographic disadvantages. Although this part of Germany had been strong in the manufacture of optical and precision instruments, textiles, cellulose, paper goods, and chemicals, the iron and steel industry was located in Western Germany and those territories that were turned over to Poland at the end of the war. Under Hitler and before, the part of Germany which now makes up the GDR had accounted for less than one-fourth of the Reich's heavy equipment, motor vehicle, machine, and electrical manufacturing.

By any standard this would have meant a poor beginning. But in addition to these disadvantages East Germany also had to pay the major share of the penalty for the Reich's defeat.

A West German economist, Professor Fritz Baade of Kiel University, once said, "No one can deny that Germans as a whole owed a debt to the Soviet Union for the senseless destruction caused there. The bill, however, has been paid by East Germany alone. On the day of reunification the eastern half of Germany will be legitimately entitled to present a demand for millions in reparations which we should have helped to pay."

The amount does not come to millions but to billions.

Between May 1945 and 1953 the Soviets carted off some 45 per cent of East Germany's total prewar industrial equipment, in addition to approximately 20 per cent that had been destroyed during the war. Whatever the Russians failed to dismantle they turned into Soviet corporations that produced goods and profits solely for Soviet benefit at a loss of approximately $1 billion to the East German economy. In addition, during the first postwar decade, East Germany had to pay the Soviet Union $10 billion in direct reparations: cash, finished products, and occupation costs.

East Germany's economy was plagued by other troubles as well during the postwar years. At the height of the Cold War numerous Western intelligence agencies waged industrial and economic sabotage against East Germany. Then too there was the mass exodus of East Germany's labor force.

Many economists have tried to calculate the monetary meaning to the GDR of these various physical, industrial, and human losses, when measured against the aid received by West Germany. The most reliable analysis was made by Professor Hans Apel, formerly of Bridgeport University in Connecticut. Apel totted up everything. He figured out what the human exodus cost East Germany, how much West Germany gained from these refugees, how much West Germany had to spend to house and integrate them, how much East Germany saved on housing construction and social welfare as a result of the drain. He took into account that West Germany received $3.8 billion from the US, but that unlike the GDR it has also paid out billions in restitution to Israel and to individual Jewish victims of Nazism. He also figured out that losses incurred during the first five years after the war inflicted greater damage on East Germany's economy than those during the decade 1951 to 1960.

The result of this complicated computation: compared to West Germany, the GDR piled up a handicap of $26.7 billion from 1945 through 1960.

No wonder it took the GDR so much longer to recover, no wonder it is still so much poorer than the FRG.

But there was another factor, too—economic bungling by the Communist leadership. For the first eighteen years after the war, East Germany practiced Soviet-Stalinist-style central planning and management. Everything was decided at the top. The managers of state-owned factories were given a plan to fulfill. It emphasized quantity not quality and paid almost no attention to whether the goods produced were in demand or did anyone any good. Managers were told by the ministries in East Berlin not only how many pieces or tons of a given product to manufacture, but how many supplies, raw materials, parts, workers, how much in wages, how much in investment they were to put into making it. They literally received instructions on the number of nuts and bolts they could put into making a tractor, how many buttons to sew on a shirt, how many nails to hammer into a packing crate.

In practice this was madness. When a construction materials plant discovered it would fail to meet its goal for producing a certain number of bricks, it just started baking them 10 per cent smaller to save materials. When a factory making men's pajamas realized it would not have enough material to meet the production target, it just cut the sleeves and pants legs a few inches shorter.

This was also the era when manufacturers tried to make the heaviest machinery possible because the plan measured success by weight instead of quality, usefulness or sales potential. One result: East German locomotive transmissions weighed four times as much as similar but more efficient ones made in West Germany.

These were terrible times when the only color in East German life came from the red propaganda posters that hung from public buildings, when even funeral parlors solemnly pledged to fulfill "the plan" by burying more people than they had the year before.

The turning points came in the late 1950s and early 60s.

First came a decision by the Russians in 1957 to stop milking and start helping East Germany. The Soviet Union agreed to deliver vast amounts of raw materials and semi-finished goods such as hard coal, coke, iron ore, pig iron, and sheet metal. It also gave the GDR a $350 million loan.

The second step was forced collectivization of agriculture. The decision to put an end to private farming in East Germany in 1960 was a political one. Private farming, in Ulbricht's view, just did not fit into a socialist society in which manufacturing and trade were state run. But it also made economic sense, for East Germany had never been and would never be self-sufficient in agriculture and had, like West Germany, one of the most inefficient farming economies in the world. In 1939 only 2.5 per cent of Germany's farms had been larger than 125 acres. Some 56 per cent ranged from 1.25 to 12.5 acres in size, the rest were smaller than one acre. Small as most plots were, however, the majority of farmers refused to turn them over to the collectives which started to organize as early as 1952. They were independent-minded and wanted to remain masters of their own land. In 1960 the regime decided to force them into collective farming. It was a terrible campaign of pressure, intimidation, blackmail, imprisonment, and outright force, but unlike similar drives in other Communist countries, it produced results. Instead of going down, East German agricultural production has climbed steadily since 1960. The GDR today is the most efficient agricultural country in the Communist world and obtains yields from marginal land that are almost as good as those obtained in the richest agricultural countries of Western Europe. Moreover the overwhelming majority of farmers now approve of the collective system. It has raised their standard of living to a par with that of skilled industrial workers—a level which no German farmer would have dreamed of in the 1930s.

The third step was the building of the Berlin Wall in 1961.

The fourth event was the introduction of economic reform, called the New Economic System. This put the emphasis on quality instead of quantity, on decentralization of the decision-making process, on incentives and bonuses, on efficiency, and on profitability. The new catchwords were science, know-how, and technology. The number and weight of tractors to be produced was no longer important.

What counted was how good they were, how competitive they might be on world markets, how efficient on the domestic scene, and how much the state could reap in profits from them.

As a young executive in a state-owned chemical plant once said to me, explaining the new system, "The only thing that distinguishes us from managers in the West is that the profit we make goes to the state and eventually the people, instead of a clique of absentee owners or a small group of shareholders. Our goals, our methods, our worries differ little, if at all, from those of an American or West German company official. Except, unfortunately, that we still have a little more red tape through which to cut."

This system was the beginning of East Germany's own economic miracle.

Today the GDR has the highest standard of living in the Communist world. Its gross national product grows faster each year than Britain's, Italy's, Russia's, or even America's and just about as fast as West Germany's. It ranks among the world's top ten producers of electric power, artificial gas, chemical fibers, fertilizers, plastics, synthetic rubber, railway freight cars, radio and TV receivers, household appliances, industrial machinery, machine tools, and optical and precision instruments. Since 1945 the GDR, which depends on anthracite coal from neighboring Poland and oil, natural gas, and ores from the Soviet Union, has built a dozen major power plants, fifteen iron and steel mills, ten huge chemical plants, a dozen machine tool factories, seven new electrotechnical and optical plants, four shipyards, eight cement works, and the world's only plant in which soft brown lignite can be turned into coke for steel-making.

It exports computers, cameras, automobiles, farm tractors, agricultural machinery, plastics, pharmaceuticals, machine tools, X-ray equipment, typewriters, calculators, television sets, washing machines, refrigerators, and ocean freighters, tankers, and passenger ships.

In fact, the GDR which started without a port is now one of the world's major shipbuilding and seafaring nations, with a fleet of 194 ships totaling 1.5 million tons. Two decades ago the GDR's ship line consisted of one rusty, leaky coastal freighter. The port of Rostock was literally gouged out of the earth by thousands of volunteer workers, most of them students and members of the Free German Youth organization.

With less than half a percent of the world's total population, East Germany produces almost two per cent of the world's wealth each year. No wonder East Germans are proud of their achievements and consider their own economic recovery even more miraculous than West Germany's.

"What we have today," a young executive of Rostock's state-owned shipbuilding trust told me, "we built with the sweat of our brows and the callouses of our hands. Without help from anyone. It may not compare with West Germany, but it is pretty good. People live well and the outlook is that they will live better from year to year. Of course it's been rough. And we're still not over the hump. But just look at what we had to invest to even provide a basis for an independent economy.

"Go out to the yard and look at the ships we're building. But keep in mind that in 1945 there was nothing there but grass. This part of the old Reich used to produce 4 per cent of the ships. Now we're one of the world's leaders."

And who owns all of this?

In theory, the people. In practice, the state. East German industry is run by several thousand "people's owned enterprises," abbreviated as VEB in German. These are organized in eighty "associations of people's owned enterprises," or VVBs. Each VVB is like a huge, powerful trust, comparable in many ways to a large American conglomerate or monopoly such as American Telephone and Telegraph Company, and covers a specific branch of manufacturing and distributing such as shipbuilding, optical and precision instruments, pharmaceuticals, furniture, and office machines, etc. They do their own advertising, marketing, price-setting, and research and development.

One of the strangest things about East Germany, however, is that until mid-1972 some 8,800 small businesses were either privately owned or run by private entrepreneurs in partnership with the state. They employed about 15 per cent of the country's industrial labor force and accounted for roughly 14 per cent of its industrial output. All other Communist countries had ended this kind of private enterprise by about 1960. In the summer of 1972 the East German regime began putting pressure on its private factory owners to sell out to the state. By fall most of them had, and East German industry is now virtually entirely state-owned. The only private enterprise remaining is in the retail sales and services field. Most of these are small family-run shops and repair businesses.

Would a majority of East Germans prefer to return to private ownership and enterprise if they could? That seems doubtful. As a young East Berliner once said to me, "We have been raised in this system. It is ours and we believe in it. Yes, it might be advantageous to make more of retail trade and services private for the sake of efficiency. But industry and wholesaling should remain state-run and farming should remain collective. The system has accomplished miracles. It has brought us from far behind. My generation trusts in it. We know that life here can only get better."

Will it ever get as good as it is in West Germany? That is hard to say. From 1961 to 1970 the GDR's annual growth rate was faster than West Germany's and it came from behind to close the gap. But since then both countries have been developing at about the same pace. East Germany, with one-fourth the population, now has a gross national product about one-fourth that of West Germany's.

But whether or not East Germany continues to close the gap, East Germans are—and have a right to be—proud of their accomplishments.

1
Two Worlds

The tallest structure in either Germany is East Berlin's 1,200-foot television tower. Located at Alexander Platz in what was prewar Berlin's commercial heart, it is the GDR's pride. A slender, concrete spire rising to the sky with a huge sphere at the tip, Berliners—both East and West—call it "Ulbricht's Wagging Finger." It has also been described, more accurately, as a giant-sized smokestack with an economy-sized onion on top.

Inside the onion is East Germany's smartest and most expensive restaurant. It is a good place to eat. It is also the perfect place from which to get a bird's-eye view of two worlds, especially at night.

Look from here toward West Berlin's fashionable and elegant Kurfürstendamm and you will see an ocean of light.

Alexander Platz, East Berlin's showplace

Look to the east and you will see a city half wrapped in darkness.

West Germany is a consumer-oriented society of the hard sell variety. Brightly lit shop windows compete for public attention with a kaleidoscope of flashing neon signs. East Germany is a country of recurring power shortages.

No matter how often I go to East Germany, this darkness always strikes me again, as does the general drabness and shabbiness of the cities and towns, especially the medium-sized and smaller ones off the beaten tourist and propaganda path. But after a day or so my eyes and my mind get used to it. I start to see and think in East German terms and after a while, forget that the GDR is still a much poorer country than the Federal Republic.

I have mentioned this sensation to a number of East Germans and have gotten some surprising reactions, especially from those who are free to travel to the FRG. They too feel this way, when they go to West Germany—only it is the brightness that bothers them.

"It's too showy, too garish," one East Berliner explained. "When I go to the West the bright lights, the tinsel, the gleam of newness on everything hurt my eyes. I usually need about 24 hours to get used to it."

To really compare the two Germanys and their way of life is not easy. It is made doubly difficult by the fact that West Germany seems to become more un-German with every passing day while East Germany has resisted the march of time, coming closest to what might be described as typically German in appearance and life style.

Of course, West Germany is different from America. City streets are narrower and not so straight. There is less advertising, a greater variety of small specialty shops, and the traffic seems noisier and less orderly because there is not the space to absorb it. The move to suburbia is just beginning. As a result the downtown areas of large cities—63 with a population of 100,000 or more—pulsate with life not just during business hours but at night and on weekends too. People, however, do not rush quite as much and appear to enjoy life more.

Culture and the arts play an especially important role in the lives of Germans. More than eighty cities have state-supported opera houses and even more have repertory theaters which give professional performances nightly during a season that is usually ten months long. In fact, it has been said that going to the opera, theater, or a concert is as popular among West Germans as going to a baseball or football game is to Americans. Music is a tradition that is deeply rooted in Germany and goes back well into the early seventeenth century. Youngsters are raised with the "three B's" of Bach, Beethoven, and Brahms.

All that is not to say that West Germans are not sports minded. On the contrary. Soccer, or *Fussball* as it is called in German, is a national mania. All the major cities have professional and semiprofessional teams with huge stadiums that seat from 80,000 to 100,000 people. And toward season's end, in the spring, when a team like Munich's Bayern Football Club plays Dortmund's Borussia or Essen's Black-White tangles with the team from Kaiserslautern it seems as though the entire country is glued to television sets.

Germans place more value on the old and historic; they try to preserve traditions.

The Sunday walk—sometimes almost a hike—is as much a part of life as the afternoon coffee and cake session. In Bavaria there are more than 4,000 amateur brass bands whose members have been taught to read music by their fathers and who, colorfully costumed in green hunter's jackets and leather pants with leather suspenders, play at weddings, funerals, beer festivals, and Saturday night dances. Even the corner tavern and the village inn, where men spend interminable hours playing a card game called Skat and drinking more beer than their wives approve of, are still very much a part of the scene.

The villages, especially in Bavaria, Lower Saxony, Schleswig-Holstein, and parts of Hesse and Württemberg with their half-timbered houses, steep tiled roofs, painted façades, narrow twisting streets and market squares seem almost as quaint and picturesque as they look in travel folder illustrations.

There are still castles and vineyards on the Rhine and splendid Baroque churches and monasteries in Bavaria. The famous Cologne cathedral still stands; the medieval wall surrounding Nuremberg has been completely rebuilt; Charlemagne's tomb remains untouched in Aachen; Beethoven's house stands unchanged in Bonn, and St. Paul's Church, where the 1848 parliament met, continues to be one of the sights of Frankfurt. In Munich you can still see women wearing dirndls and men in leather breeches. Fraternity students really duel and sing old drinking songs in Heidelberg. Mainz remains famous for its annual carnival parade and Hamburg for being Europe's most sinful harbor town.

West Germany is still different from America, that is true. But how much longer?

West Germans themselves already call Frankfurt "our little Chicago" and seem as proud of its forest of steel-and-glass skyscrapers as they are worried about it being a capital of crime. More quickly than they realize or want to know, theirs is becoming a country of superhighways, shopping centers, suburban living, split-level houses, laundromats, dishwashers, two-car garages, keeping up with the Joneses, TV dinners, crowded schools, unbreathable air, polluted rivers and lakes, nervous tension, ulcers and heart attacks, urban ghettos, and spiraling crime rates.

Even the typical German seems to be going the way of the dodo bird. He drinks less beer and eats fewer dumplings and enrolls in *trim dich fit* courses to keep his waistline down. His wife spurns calorie-rich cakes with whipped cream and joins weight-watcher clubs. As Vera Elyashiv, an Israeli journalist of German-Jewish parentage, wrote on her first visit a decade ago, "German men seem to look like North Italians and all wear Italian-made suits and shoes. The women appear French and prefer clothes from Paris. Their children all look like little Americans and wear blue jeans."

"But when you are in East Germany," noted Amos Elon, another Israeli journalist of similar background, "it appears as if the war ended only yesterday."

Compared with the neon-lighted superabundance of the West, East Germany appears to have stood still since the 1930s. The Saxons and Thuringians, the Brandenburgers and the Mecklenburgers seem to live in a world gone by. Unlike West Germans whose society tends to become more and more American and whose habits and tastes are being formed by travel abroad, East Germans have preserved much of the life style of prewar times. Outwardly the GDR is somehow far more German than the FRG, and for the nostalgic visitor it is an almost unspoiled spot in which to revive memories of the "good old days," even if those were not as good as they sound.

Of course, the centers of the biggest cities which were destroyed during the war—East Berlin, Leipzig, Dresden, Karl-Marx-Stadt, and Magdeburg—have been rebuilt. They

148

*A bustling street in West Germany (above)
contrasts with a nearly deserted East German street.*

display the same steel-concrete-glass construction that makes so much of West Germany faceless. And each year there are more shops and better merchandise, more advertising, more traffic, but there is also more pollution and more crime—in other words, all the benefits and disadvantages of the affluent society.

But to understand what East Germany is all about, one must keep in mind that only eleven of its cities have populations of 100,000 or more and that only 22 per cent of the people (compared with 27 per cent in the US and 33 per cent in West Germany) live in them. For the vast majority of East Germans "home" is a Mecklenburg hamlet, a Thuringian village, or one of the hundreds of small, grimy Saxonian manufacturing towns.

There life is grim and austere, dull and shabby, dusty and sooty. Joys are few, hopes even less. They were never really cheerful places. Most of them are products of the nineteenth century's industrial revolution, monuments to that century's architectural ugliness. Too unimportant to be bombed or fought over during the war, they have persevered through the peace. Little has changed, except that time and neglect have chipped the gray plaster from the brick walls of their old houses and potholed their cobblestone streets. They have become strongholds of the past.

There life retreats behind the shutters at dusk. A big night out means going to the stuffy, airless movie house to see a film with more propaganda in it than entertainment. At the most it means a dance at the town's only inn or café where couples shuffle aimlessly across the floor as a tired band plays the out-of-tune hits of yesteryear's Saturday nights.

To people living in these towns the new department stores and comfortable restaurants on East Berlin's Alexander Platz are almost as remote as New York's Fifth Avenue. It will be many more decades, if ever, before these cheerless towns change. They are one reason why for years to come East Germany will lack the Federal Republic's newness and glitter.

But that is not the only reason. West Germany's sparkle is the result of an economic system that must sell fashion, obsolescence, and status appeal to survive. In many respects it is a system in which invention becomes the mother of necessity. East Germany's rulers, on the other hand, while insisting that they favor beauty of design, good styling, and a choice of merchandise, are opposed to the principle of artificially created desire or the production of something new just for the sake of its newness. These pages are not the place to debate whether human happiness depends on the purchase of new cars, furniture, appliances, and clothing because new styles have hit the market, or whether consumption should be dictated by the fact that old things have worn out. But we cannot get around the fact that appeal to the consumer provides much of the overabundance that makes West Germany look more affluent than the GDR. East Germany, having renounced conspicuous consumption in principle, is unlikely ever to match the glitter of the West.

Nevertheless, since the building of the Berlin Wall and the upsurge in the economy, the GDR has been closing the consumer goods gap. It now boasts 71 television sets per 100 families, compared to 99 in West Germany; 69 refrigerators per 100 homes compared to 91 in the FRG; 58 washing machines per 100 households compared to 81 in the Federal Republic. East Germans now take modern and attractively styled furniture, an array of household appliances, fashionable and well-made clothing, and a comfortable home or apartment for granted. They eat almost as well as West Germans. They are shopping more discriminately and demand a selection which their state-owned industry is now prepared to provide.

The GDR is also becoming motorized. True, the cheapest car, the Trabant, still costs 7,800 marks, the equivalent of nine months' wages for the average industrial worker, compared to the four months a West German would have to work to buy the cheapest model Volkswagen. Moreover, waiting lists for this little puddle jumper are still four years long. The Trabant would not win any beauty or design contests and it leaves plenty of comfort and safety questions unanswered. Loud and only slightly larger than the smallest Fiat, its engine delivers only 27 horsepower and has a top speed of only 63 miles per hour. But it is robust, simply made, and cheap to operate, using one gallon of gas (at $1.40) per 35 miles. Called the "plastic bombshell," its body is made of a corrosion-free synthetic named "toroplast." An East German invention, the formula for which is secret, toroplast is so sturdy that three men jumping on a Trabant roof cannot dent it. It is also cheap. A replacement fender costs only $4.00.

The GDR now produces nearly 100,000 Trabants a year plus 40,000 Wartburgs, a larger more comfortable automobile costing twice as much. In addition it imports cars from Czechoslovakia, Poland, and the Soviet Union. At the end of 1972 there were 74 passenger cars per 1,000 inhabitants compared to 255 in West Germany, and 446 in the United States. This may not seem many, but ownership has doubled since 1967, and the ratio is higher than in Israel or Czechoslovakia, not to mention the Soviet Union where there are 5 cars per 1,000 population.

Although consumer goods are a legitimate indicator of

living standards, they do not tell anywhere near the entire story.

Let's examine some of the other factors.

West Germany is and looks richer because, proportionally, there are almost three times as many West Germans as East Germans in the top income bracket, that is, family groups of 3.5 people with monthly net earnings of 2,000 marks or more. Moreover that top bracket in West Germany includes not only the well-to-do but the rich and the super rich.

With the exception of some writers, entertainers, academics, scientists, senior executives, and top government and party officials, East Germany has almost no people who could be called rich. Those East Germans who are in the top category, however, live approximately as well as their counterparts in the Federal Republic.

A well-known East German couple, he a construction engineer, she the GDR's most successful architect and city planner, have a joint monthly income of 4,000 marks. They have two children, own a modern single-family house, have two Wartburg cars, all the appliances and gadgets they could need, and a valuable collection of antiques. They live no differently and certainly no worse than a West German family with the same income.

From 1970 until the end of 1973 the earnings of West German blue- and white-collar workers increased by more than 30 per cent. But during those four years West Germany also faced an average annual inflation rate of 7 per cent plus hikes in taxes and social security payments that soaked up most of those wage and salary rises. In terms of actual spending power, a West German factory worker had only slightly more in 1973 than in 1970.

Although wages increased by only 10 per cent in East

Germany during the same four-year period, government-controlled prices remained absolutely stable and tax increases were minimal. As a result the East Germans have been closing the gap.

A very important factor is the contribution made to family incomes by East German women.

More than 84 per cent of all East German women work, compared to only 53 per cent in West Germany. A larger proportion of them work full time and their pay is more equal to that of men and therefore relatively higher than in West Germany. Female earnings thus make up an important chunk of the net family income, which in 1973 was around 1,200 marks per month compared to about 1,500 in West Germany.

In many respects real comparisons between the two countries cannot be made because conditions, standards, and values are so different. For example, although East Germans must work two to four times longer than West Germans for certain consumer durables such as cars and appliances, basic commodities and services in East Germany are often much cheaper than in the Federal Republic. Rent for an apartment consumes about 25 per cent of the average West German family's income but never more than 10 per cent of an East German family's. In fact, rents in East Germany are so low that landlords, private or government, cannot afford upkeep costs. That is one reason why East German cities and towns look so shabby and drab. Whereas East Germans pay five times more for certain luxury goods such as coffee and alcohol, West Germans shell out five to six times more than East Germans for services such as public transport, haircuts, and entertainment. West Germans may earn more money and have more in the bank, but East Germany offers more security. The average

East German old-age pension is only one-third as high as in West Germany, but its purchasing power for basic commodities and services is almost the same.

"People value the security of this system," a top executive in the GDR's chemical industry once told me. "The state rewards the hard worker, but it also protects those who cannot or do not work so hard. Western businessmen have asked me why I don't defect to the Federal Republic where I could get a position paying 10 to 20 times what I earn here. Frankly, I'm afraid I wouldn't make out in the competitive jungle of the capitalist world. And if I did, at what price? A heart attack? Our pace is slower, we take it easier. That may be one reason why we are behind, but I wouldn't trade."

The prevailing attitude in East Germany is that the system makes the future safe. Inflation, stock market crashes, unemployment, economic fluctuations, long illnesses—those are all problems with which the East German need not concern himself. Many East Germans raise these points when explaining why, despite West Germany's higher standard of living, they would prefer to live in the GDR.

"I know what I've got here," an assembly-line worker in the Trabant automobile factory once told me. "It may not be as much as in West Germany. But where's the guarantee that in the FRG I wouldn't be selling apples on the street some day? It happened once in Germany, so who's to say it can't happen again?"

Because the majority of East Germans can watch West German television broadcasts which reach all but the southeastern corner of the country, they are surprisingly well informed about conditions in the Federal Republic. They are outspoken both about what they accept and what they reject.

"As far as consumer goods and living standards go," said a woman in Hoyerswerda, a Saxonian industrial town, "I know we can't hold a candle to West Germany. Life is better, more joyful there. Another thing—we've got too much politics and propaganda in our lives. The party tries to inject politics into everything. Do we really have to give six-year-old kids lectures on Marxism-Leninism? But there are fewer pressures in our society, and I can tell you one thing—our kids are being raised more morally. They are better behaved, more disciplined. We don't have as many long-haired ones, and I can assure you there's no one in Hoyerswerda who smokes pot."

Both Germanys are welfare states. The Federal Republic pays lucrative family allowances to people with two children or more. The GDR offers interest-free loans and rewards them for each child born. The compulsory medical insurance system, initiated by Bismarck, is still in effect in both states with improvements and variations. Each state has its specific benefits. Most West Germans are entitled to four weeks vacation a year and at Christmas time receive an extra month's salary. East Germans take collectivized, cut-rate vacations at their factory or government-owned resort hotels for granted. Going in a group with the people on the assembly line to the mountains or beach may not be everyone's idea of a happy holiday, but it is cheap. The price—travel, board, lodging, and entertainment included—is rarely more than 10 per cent of the family's monthly income for a two-week stay.

Although Germans in both states have never lived better than they do today, and life improves from year to year, both do have problems.

The top issue in West Germany in the early 1970s was spiralling inflation mixed with rising government spending and increased taxes. The Federal Republic's inflation rate has not been the worst in the world or in Europe. But the fact is that a Deutsche mark in 1973 bought only 63 per cent of what it had ten years earlier. The government has promised strict measures and drastic steps, but at the time of writing, prices are still climbing and the end is not yet in sight. When the inflation rate became higher than interest earnings on savings accounts, people stopped saving and decided to go on spending sprees, which merely drove prices higher.

What it means to the average West German was expressed by one Munich sales executive, father of two small children, whose gross monthly income is 2,500 marks. Of this he must pay out more than 1,000 marks in taxes, social security, medical, old-age and unemployment insurance premiums. Of the remaining 1,440 marks, 350 go for rent on a two-bedroom apartment, 450 for food, 250 for payments on his car, 100 for liability and collision insurance, 50 for gasoline. That leaves 240 marks for everything else, including the phone bill, utilities, clothing, furniture, acquisitions, incidentals, entertainment, and vacations. Considering that this is the equivalent of an average quality man's suit, it is very little.

"A year ago," he explained, "I was able to save 50 marks a month. This year, though we buy cheaper food and stayed home during our vacation, we still can't really make out."

In East Germany the major problem, as it has been since the 1950s, is still the shortage of certain goods and the sporadic distribution of most of them. Of course the GDR has come a long way from the days when there seemed to be nothing but left-footed shoes, right-handed gloves, mops but no handles, handles but no mops, tires without tubes, and nails but no hammers. Those were the

East German shoppers (above) *waiting to purchase scarce consumer goods;* (below) *a shopping mall in West Germany*

days when people shopped not for what they wanted but for whatever was momentarily available. The classic story of those times is about a man walking across the town square with a huge funeral wreath. A friend stops and asks him who died. "Oh, no one. But they're selling wreaths today and I thought I'd better get one to keep until I need it."

But shortages still exist and plans still go wrong. Something is usually missing somewhere, sold out yesterday or may be available tomorrow. In Dresden in August 1973, for example, the unavailable items were writing paper, toothbrushes, automobile spark plugs, clothes pins, and rubber bands. The next week pencils, toothpaste, windshield wipers, clothesline, and paper clips could have been in short supply.

The lack of choice coupled with periodic shortages of some goods and the sudden oversupply of others makes daily shopping a nerve-straining task. As one East German woman described it, "A West German or American housewife can sit down in the morning, make up a shopping list and plan her meals, then go to the supermarket and buy as much as her budget permits. But my meals are dictated by what I happen to find on the shelves. No noodles? I take rice or macaroni. No veal? Cook something with pork. There aren't real shortages as such, but I always end up shopping for what is available, not what I really want or need. You just cannot find everything all of the time and there are some things you find none of the time. I fill my pantry or my refrigerator according to the whim of some invisible planning expert in Berlin. He's the one who decides what I'm going to feed my family tonight, not I."

The smaller the town, the farther from a major highway or main railway line, the worse this problem is.

The Two Germanys

One problem that both Germanys seem to have in common is the rising crime rate. Sociologists attribute this to a variety of causes, some of which apply to both states, some to only one or the other: these are, increasing industrialization; alienation of the individual in industrial societies; emulation, especially of crimes shown in movies and on television; the impact of minority groups and the development of ghettos and slums; boredom among juveniles; and a growing gap between social and economic classes.

By West German standards East Germany is an oasis of peace and public safety, for the crime rate in the Federal Republic is six times higher than in the GDR. And by American standards both Germanys are models of law and order. In 1969, the last year for which comparative figures are available, there were fewer murders committed in all of West Germany than in the three largest US cities—New York, Chicago, and Los Angeles; fewer in East Germany than in Newark, New Jersey. West Germany recorded fewer robberies than Washington, D.C.; East Germany less than Greensboro, North Carolina. There were six times as many rapes in the United States as in West Germany, forty-five times as many as in the GDR.

But these statistics provide little comfort for German law enforcement officials, who note that crime rates in both Germanys have been rising steadily at about 10 per cent since 1968 and at an even sharper pace in the large cities.

By 1980, says Hans-Werner Hammacher, Cologne's chief of detectives and one of the Federal Republic's top crime experts, uniformed police will be riding guard in West German subway trains just as they do in America, the murder rate will have doubled, and armed robberies and burglaries will have tripled.

The increase in East Germany is so alarming—and apparently so embarrassing to the Communist regime, which has always insisted that crime is a capitalist, not a socialist phenomenon—that the authorities decided in 1972 to stop publishing the figures. The GDR's 1973 Statistical Yearbook is the first edition in twenty-four years to leave out all statistics dealing with crime and punishment.

"It seems," said Dr. Josef Streit, the GDR's solicitor-general and chief prosecutor, "that we are going to have to approach this problem more realistically. Despite the victory of socialism in our country, there are still great differences of development between social classes and strong remnants of capitalist morality."

In West Germany, where capital punishment was abolished in 1949, the increase in murders has spurred a move to bring the death penalty back. In the fall of 1971 when a sex deviate who had killed three young girls was sentenced in court, irate spectators shouted, "We need Hitler back." "Chop his head off."

"Harsher penalties," said one West German law enforcement official, "are really not the answer. The public is going to have to realize that the increase in violent crime parallels the experience of all other industrially advanced countries. The solution is to reduce the economic and social strains that industrialization brings with it."

In many respects both Germanys have done more toward that end than most industrialized countries.

In both there is growing preoccupation with the quality of life. A great deal of attention has been paid to making the cities livable. East Germany, for example, was one of the first countries in the world to establish a ministry for environmental protection and many of the West German states, led by Bavaria, followed suit.

Downtown areas of large cities in both Germanys have

been turned into pedestrian malls, and there is a conscious attempt to preserve the inner cities as places where people not only work but live and entertain themselves. Municipal parks are still areas where people can relax after work and on weekends without fear of being robbed or mugged.

Vast amounts of public and private money have been invested in providing better housing in both Germanys.

"The problem of rising crime rates," a West German mayor once explained to me, 'is closely linked to the dehumanization of life in the big cities of the industrial countries. Neither the Communist nor the Capitalist system has a patented solution for dealing with it. But if we can recognize the cause we are halfway toward solving the problem."

8
Women : The New Majority

German society, more than any other in Europe, was traditionally patriarchal—a world in which stern, strong men ruled autocratically while the domain of women was restricted to the "three K's" of *Kinder, Kirche, Küche*—children, cooking, and church. Adolf Hitler did more to promote this image of a world dominated by males and father figures than any German ruler before him.

It is ironic that Hitler's war changed all that.

Between 1939 and 1945 more than 20 million German males were called to arms. Before the war was over nearly 10 million men had been killed, wounded and maimed, or taken prisoner. Millions of women became the sole breadwinners of their families, and when the guns stopped shooting it was the women of Germany who cleared the rubble of the wrecked cities and began the country's reconstruction.

The war changed the traditional role of German women. It left them in the majority and was the start of their liberation process.

That process is more advanced in East than in West Germany. But despite enormous disparities between the GDR and FRG, the women of both Germanys today are more liberated, enjoy more rights, and have more influence on society as a whole than women anywhere else in the world. And they remain very much in the majority. They outnumber men by 3 million in the West and by 1.5 million in the GDR. The constitutions of both Germanys state specifically that men and women have equal rights. East Germany's even goes so far as to say that the "advancement of women, in particular professionally, is an obligation of society and the state."

But the process of their emancipation is far from completed and despite the fact that women are in the majority, they do not rule.

The cause of the trouble may be that although both Germanys now have a new kind of woman, they both still have the old kind of man.

One of them is the FRG's former Chancellor Kurt Georg Kiesinger who once said, "Women should be reserved in regard to politics so that they will be able to reduce the enormous importance that men attach to it in daily life." Another is the Bavarian political leader Franz-Josef Strauss who says flatly: "I cannot persuade myself that more women should be active in politics."

Very few are. Although there are 3.5 million more female than male voters registered in West Germany, only 6 out of 1,000 women, compared to 40 men, are dues-paying mem-

bers of a political party. A number of women play important roles in government, but the impression of token-
ism is hard to dispel. Thus, the minister of health, youth,
and family affairs is a woman, Katharina Focke, but she is
the only one in Chancellor Schmidt's cabinet of 15. The
president of the Bundestag, a position equal to that of the
speaker of the US House of Representatives, is Annemarie
Renger. Yet the number of female deputies in the Bundestag has decreased steadily since 1949 and by 1973 there
were only 29 out of a total membership of 496. The official
explanation: "The cares and hardships of the early postwar
years led to a greater commitment among women. In the
recent, more affluent period, women have been more concerned with bringing up their children. Fewer qualified
women politicians are rising from the grass roots political
level."

The picture in East Germany looks only somewhat better.
True, 13 per cent of East Germany's mayors and 34 per
cent of its judges are women. Women play a significant role
in city, county, and district councils, and their representation in the Volkskammer has increased steadily since 1949
to the point where there are now 159 female deputies, or
more than 30 per cent of the total membership. But as in
West Germany there is only one woman in the cabinet,
Honecker's wife, Margot, who serves as minister of education. Moreover, women play almost no role in those places
where the real power lies in the GDR—the leadership or-
gans of the Socialist Unity party. Although women account
for 29 per cent of the SED's total membership, their representation on the Central Committee is only 13 per cent.
Two women, Margarete Müller and Inge Lange, are nonvoting "candidate members" of the Politburo, but its 16
full members are all men. There is but one woman, Inge

Annemarie Renger, president of the Bundestag

Lange, in the all-powerful party Secretariat, and she did not join it until October 1973, the first woman in twenty-seven years of the party's existence to do so.

Compared to the US and other West European countries, women in the Federal Republic play a larger role in the professions and business life, but in relation to men, it is still a minor one. Only 3 per cent of the judges and a mere 4 per cent of the university-level instructors are women, although women account for almost 25 per cent of the college and university enrollment. Some of West Germany's top journalists are women, among them Countess Marion Dönhoff, the editor-in-chief of *Die Zeit,* the largest and most influential weekly newspaper; the chief financial and business correspondent of one TV network; and the political editor of the largest regional network. But the press corps in Bonn is predominantly male. Of the nearly 10 million working women, more than 700,000 are self-employed. But only 6 per cent of working women, compared to 25 per cent of the men, are in the top two salary brackets. The reason: "Many women work only part time and many do not have the qualifications needed for the better paying jobs." That, at least, is the official explanation for the fact that men, on the average, bring home 50 per cent more pay than women. But it is also true that those who do have the skills and who do work full time are generally paid less, even when doing the same job.

Less than 2 per cent of West Germany's top corporate executives are women, and the female representation on the boards of directors of large companies is almost too small to count: one-tenth of one per cent. Explaining this phenomenon, the chairman of one of West Germany's largest breweries said, "But that is only logical. Women, for example, do not drink very much beer, so there would be no place on our board for a woman."

In 1969 the Bundestag passed a law designed to help women, especially housewives who want to return to work after a homemaking, child-rearing absence from the labor market, to acquire the skills that will qualify them for higher paying jobs. It provides for government cash grants and tuition for training and retraining courses.

In East Germany women also take home less money than men, though the discrepancy is nowhere near as great. The GDR's economy is so desperately short of labor and has so few foreign reserves to draw on that it would break down completely without the women who work. To free them from the apron strings, the regime has offered persuasive inducements ranging from complete equality on the job, including equal wages, to inexpensive, scientifically run childcare centers and eighteen weeks maternity leave at full pay plus 1,000 marks in cash during pregnancy.

Women are everywhere and do everything. They rivet, manage chemical plants, drive bulldozers, operate streetcars and trains, regulate traffic, design dams, run power plants, hospitals, schools, collective farms, and preside over courts. Nevertheless, there is discrimination. It merely takes a different form.

The cause in part is biological. Women bear the children even in Communist societies. Having a baby entitles a woman to more than four months' leave. This disrupts the procedure in any enterprise, and the more qualified a woman and the more important her duties, the more disruptive the effect is. Consequently many plant managers have a built-in prejudice against women in crucial jobs. The GDR's satirical weekly, *Eulenspiegel,* described this problem in a cartoon a number of years ago. "I'll have to give

In East Germany, women are a vital part of the work force.

the job to Paul," said a factory chief, pointing to a some-what stupid-looking man while smiling apologetically at a bright young woman applicant with a big diploma under her arm. "He may not have a degree, but he'll never get pregnant."

There is a conflict of course between woman's produc-tive and reproductive role, and it would be ostrich-like to ignore it. The GDR now has enough day-care centers and nurseries to accommodate 30 per cent of all children up to age three and enough preschools to take care of 70 per cent of those between three and six. All of them are models of child care where toddlers are supervised by trained teach-ers, cared for scientifically, fed perfectly balanced meals, examined monthly by dentists and pediatricians, and taught group living in clean and modern surroundings.

But East German experts on child raising are not at all sure whether this program is a good idea. The effect of it may well be an entire generation of neurotics raised with-out parental love. As one doctor in the GDR told me in private conversation, "Kids, no matter how young, are sub-consciously aware of the love they receive or don't receive. The children dumped with strangers each day must sense they are in someone's way and they are likely to grow up accordingly. Moreover, being raised in such surroundings has a retarding effect. We can recognize immediately which children have been raised in day nurseries, which ones have grown up at home. The ones from preschools are, comparatively speaking, retarded. They have been sys-tematically deprived of the impulses they receive in adult surroundings. No matter how good the teachers and super-visors, they cannot devote the time to influencing each child as intensively as its mother. With no adults around them for most of the day, they do not learn, they copy each other." To raise these points in public in the GDR is taboo, however, largely because mothers are so vital to the production process.

Husbands are another part of the problem in East Germany. When questioned, they all proclaim that they do not object to their wives working. But the majority still expect their women to take care of the household as well.

One recent study disclosed that although 74 per cent of East German men with working wives do some chores in the house, the lion's share still falls to the wives. Thus, 84 per cent of the cooking, 78 per cent of the cleaning, 90 per cent of the laundering, and 76 per cent of the shopping is left to the woman.

How little things have really changed was revealed in a survey among East German first-graders who were asked to describe what their mothers and fathers do. Mother, according to most of the kids, "cooks the meals, does the shopping, mops the floor, washes the clothes, and sews on buttons." Father "reads books and newspapers, watches television, drinks beer, and smokes cigarettes."

"Unless we succeed in revolutionizing family relationships, that is, getting the husbands to darn socks and do a few other things occasionally," said one woman engineer, "nothing will really change and our new opportunities will be no more than paper promises."

Male reluctance to help in the home is mentioned as a factor in more than half of the divorce cases in East Germany, and considering that the divorce rate in the GDR is 50 per cent higher than in West Germany, East German women must really have something to complain about.

On the other hand, the GDR's divorce and family relations law, in effect since April 1966, is a milestone of progress. Very similar legislation was introduced in the

West German Bundestag in August 1973, but at the time of writing was still bogged down in committee and not expected to come to a final vote for another year.

The East German law revolutionized traditional relationships between men and women, literally freeing wives from the indenture of the apron strings. It specifies that both partners in marriage are responsible for the children and for running the household. That means, in theory, that a working wife could legally require her husband to help with the dishes. This is the complete opposite of traditional West German law which empowers a husband to force his wife to the kitchen sink, even if she is willing to pay for domestic help from her own earnings. Under the old West German code the husband must assume the principal burden of financial support for the family, the woman primary responsibility for keeping house.

East German law also entitles women to retain their own names after marriage and men to take the last names of their wives and both, if they wish, to hyphenate and use the two names.

Another crucial step toward emancipation of East German women was the March 1972 legalization of abortion. The law entitles women to abortion on demand, without cost, during the first three months of pregnancy. Similar legislation is in preparation in West Germany, but has not yet been introduced in the Bundestag. A decree accompanying the abortion law made oral contraceptives available free of charge to all females aged sixteen or older.

The male-female relationship is one of the biggest issues in both Germanys today. In the GDR the discussion focuses not only on employment opportunities, pay, and division of household duties, but who is entitled to be the more aggressive partner. The biggest box-office hit in years in the GDR was a movie called *The Third* in which a successful woman computer analyst, mother of two fatherless daughters, likes a man she has seen but feels too inhibited to make the first move toward him. "Here I am," she says in the crucial scene, "supposedly emancipated and yet social custom says I'd make a fool of myself by telling a man I want him." In the end, of course, she does precisely that, winning a father for her two children.

"We've been discussing a similar problem in class," one teenager told an East German newspaper reporter. "The question is why only boys should ask girls out to dance and not the other way around."

There is, in fact, only one burning women's liberation topic that is not discussed in either Germany: whether to address a woman as Miss, Mrs., or Ms. Language and the peculiarities of politics have a lot to do with that. The German word for both "woman" and "wife" is *Frau*. That is also the title of a married woman. Unmarried, she is a *Fräulein*, which is both a title and a description, for it means a "little woman." It is customary, however, to address all mature women, whether married or not, as Frau and at age forty all unmarried women are legally entitled to that address. In one survey, 58 per cent of unmarried women over thirty preferred to be called Frau, 19 per cent opted for Fräulein, and the rest said they did not care one way or the other.

In East Germany the problem hardly comes up at all, for both titles have been more or less abolished. Everyone is a "Comrade." The only difference is that a woman, regardless of age or marital state, is called a *Genossin*, while a man is a *Genosse*. Emancipation cannot change the rules of grammar, but it seems to me that that is about as equal as you can get.

9
The New Generation

Since 1945 a huge question mark has come to replace the swastika as the symbol of Germany. And nearly everyone asks: Have the Germans really changed?

It is a legitimate question to raise about a people who twice within one lifetime plunged mankind into the most devastating wars in history and who, as a nation, share guilt for the murder of millions.

But then one must also ask: Who are the Germans today? More than 7 million East Germans and nearly 27 million West Germans—about 43 per cent of the populations of both Germanys—are now under thirty years of age. That means they were born after World War II had ended. Can they also be blamed for the Second and Third Reich or for the failure of democracy during the Weimar Republic?

Do they—could they even—have anything in common with the hundreds of thousands of uniformed, starry-eyed Hitler Youths who shouted "*Sieg Heil*" at Nazi party rallies a generation ago? With the millions of Wehrmacht soldiers who obediently jackbooted across West and East Europe? With the thousands—many of them teenagers barely out of school—who served as concentration camp guards?

Hardly. Those marching multitudes of the 1930s and 1940s were the grandparents and parents of today's young Germans, between whom there is the biggest generation gap the world has ever known. As Baldur von Schirach, the leader of the Hitler Youth movement, said in 1966 after being released from Spandau prison where he had served a twenty-year term for war crimes, "It would be impossible to mobilize Germany's youth today. The new generation is too smart and too skeptical to be seduced by romantic nationalism."

That evaluation, I believe, applies to the new generation in both Germanys despite the fact that their views were formed by completely different approaches to dealing with the Nazi past, by different educational systems, and strikingly different environments.

Settling scores with Nazis and Nazism, re-educating German youth, and setting up safeguards to make sure something like the Hitler regime would not happen again became major tasks in both Germanys after the war. The approach varied greatly.

The Federal Republic did a great deal of official atoning. By insisting that it was the sole, legal successor to the German Reich, it also accepted the Reich's burden of guilt. However, except for the younger generation, which asks why it should be blamed for the crimes of its parents, most West Germans shrink away when faced with the mirror of their own past. They would, if they could, like to think of the Third Reich as foggy, distant ancient history. Shame makes them want to forget the past.

East Germany on the other hand shifted the entire burden of guilt into West Germany's lap by describing Nazism, not as an abnormality of German history, but as a natural outgrowth of monopoly capitalism. According to East German theory, wherever capitalism has been abolished, Nazism and its seed are dead. Arnold Zweig, the famous left-wing German-Jewish novelist who resettled in the GDR after the war, once said, "We didn't have to master or digest the past: We vomited it out."

Most East Germans tend to think of the Hitler era as West Germany's problem. They have tried to wash the common stain of Nazism down West Germany's drain. To listen to many East Germans talk you would think the GDR had been a victim, not part of the aggressor nation. While West Germany discreetly ignored the anniversaries of VE Day, May 8th became a public holiday in the GDR and is celebrated as a "day of liberation."

West Germany has paid compensation to Israel and to individual victims of Nazi persecution or their survivors, and the payments, both as lump sums and in the form of life-long pensions, are still being made. By 1975 they will have cost the Federal Republic more than $12 billion.

This East Germany refused—and still refuses—to do, contending that it carried more than a fair share of the burden in the form of reparations to the Soviet Union. Moreover, the GDR is allied with the Arabs against Israel. It has refused to compensate Jews for lost or confiscated property, on grounds that "Jewish capitalists were capitalists like all others and must not be given preferred treatment just because they are Jews."

Both Germanys prosecuted—and continue to prosecute—Nazi criminals. Although West Germany makes far more noise about it, the fact is that East Germany has done a more thorough job, though with less regard for the rules of law or the rights of the accused.

What to do with the tens of thousands of civil servants, diplomats, judges, prosecutors, policemen, teachers, and professors who had been members of the Nazi party and fellow travelers also posed major problems for both Germanys.

Konrad Adenauer did not have too many scruples about this and defended the employment of many former Nazis with the remark, "You cannot build up a professional administration or diplomatic corps with amateurs." This lax attitude toward a man's political past went so far that a former Nazi party member, Kurt Georg Kiesinger, became chancellor of the Federal Republic in 1966 and a man accused of having helped to build concentration camps, Heinrich Luebke, served two terms as its president. That was grist for the East German propaganda mill, and for many years the East Germans had a field day accusing West Germany of protecting and promoting Nazis in government.

But hunting Nazi skeletons in the other fellow's closet is a game two can play. To this day, three members of East Germany's State Council, four members of the cabinet, twelve members of the Socialist Unity party's Central Committee, and a score of other top-ranking party and government officials are former Nazis.

The ghost of the embarrassing past also haunts the two German armies. When West Germany began rearming in 1955 it tried to erase all memories of the dreaded Wehrmacht. The *Bundeswehr* was to be a "democratic army" of "citizens in uniform." The uniform itself was completely redesigned and all the old practices of Germany's Prussian militarist tradition were abolished. In fact, discipline is so lax, rules of dress, haircuts, and appearance so liberal, that the once-feared *Luftwaffe* is now jokingly called the "German Hair Force." But to make it an effective fighting team, the Bonn government drew on trained professionals—senior officers and generals who had served Hitler before 1945. The East German National People's Army, on the other hand, wears virtually the same uniform the Wehrmacht did and still practices the same ironclad drill and discipline, right down to the jackbooted goosestep that once sent shudders up and down Europe's spine. But its generals and senior officers, for the most part, are former noncoms, workers, and farmers and some even got their military training fighting on the Republican side in the Spanish Civil War. As one amused observer put it: "The FRG changed the uniform but kept the old generals. The GDR kept the old uniform but changed the generals."

The biggest dilemma facing either Germany was how to deal with the embarrassing facts of history in the schools. Neither country has really come to grips with the problem.

Until 1970 most of what West German youth knew about the Third Reich it had learned from television, movies, the press, and outside reading. The schools taught little; textbooks, many of whose authors were compromised by their own behavior during the Nazi era, said even less. The causes for Hitler's rise to power were usually whitewashed in a couple of superficial paragraphs. The crimes committed in the concentration camps sometimes filled less than a line of text. Educators were afraid to face the past because it was their own past as well. Consequently hundreds of thousands of young Germans became adults know-

Soldiers of the new West German army (above)
provide a sharp contrast to the goose-stepping East Germans.

ing little more about Hitler than that he had been "the mustached man who built the autobahns."

What the East Germans did was different but not much better. Their schools portray the Third Reich as something that happened in some remote, distant place. It is almost as if there had been two German pasts. As one GDR textbook describes it, "Hitler came to power in 1933 when industrialists, Ruhr barons, and militarists—who rule West Germany to this day—met secretly to find a front man who would implement their policies: Hitler. Their long-range goals included suppression of the Soviet Union and peace-loving German peasants and workers. They needed a terrorist reign to achieve their goals." East German young people have never been told, and probably never will be, that their own parents and grandparents cheered for Hitler and carried out his orders, or why.

It is in the field of education, in fact, that the two Germanys are most unlike, though both entered the postwar era with the same educational system rooted in the nineteenth century.

West Germany's has remained basically unchanged and has been described as nothing less than a national scandal. According to Dr. Hildegard Hamm-Brücher, West Germany's former deputy minister of science and education, now head of the Free Democratic party in Bavaria, the Federal Republic has become "an educational Appalachia." Formal schooling for the majority of West Germans is shorter than in any industrialized country—East or West—and shorter than in many of the underdeveloped nations.

East Germany's system, on the other hand, has undergone a revolution that once prompted the West German weekly *Die Zeit* to say: "It is inconceivable that the two systems had a common origin." Quantitatively the GDR is the most educated country in Europe today.

Here are a few comparative statistics.

In West Germany the ratio of pupils to teacher is more than thirty to one. In East Germany it is twenty to one. Fewer than 35 per cent of West German youth receive ten or more years of schooling, or at least the equivalent of a completed American high school education. In the GDR this group is more than 80 per cent. Fewer than 6 per cent of West German youth go on to a university, compared to more than 15 per cent in East Germany.

The number of West German universities and colleges has barely doubled since the end of the war, and space in them for students is so limited that in 1973 plans were being discussed for sending some 30,000 young West Germans to the US to study at less crowded American campuses. In East Germany the number of colleges and universities has increased ninefold since 1945 and the GDR has almost half as many students enrolled as West Germany, though its population is only one-fourth as great.

In West Germany a university education has remained more or less a privilege of the upper and upper-middle classes, while in East Germany the vast majority of college students—75 per cent—are the children of blue- and white-collar workers and farmers.

There are a number of reasons for this imbalance. One of them is the old Marxist slogan, "knowledge is power." That was the principle of the nineteenth century workers' education societies, from which both the Socialist and Communist parties originated, and was the basis of the education reform which the Ulbricht regime introduced. Its aim was to raise the general level of education, erase all class and social distinctions, and to equip as many children as possible with both theoretical and practical knowledge.

West Germany's Social Democrats also believe in the old Marxist slogan, but they have been in power only a few years, not long enough to undo more than twenty years of damage. Until 1970 the FRG spent half as much—proportionately—on education as Japan, the United States, Finland, or Czechoslovakia, less than most West or East European countries and only slightly more than such education backwaters as Turkey, Portugal, Kenya, or Ghana. It will take many years before the Federal Republic can make up the time it lost.

Most important of all, however, is that West Germany retained the basic educational system first introduced in the mid-nineteenth century. The great majority—66 per cent—of West German children receive only nine years of education at so-called *Volksschulen* from which they are graduated at age fifteen, then begin three-year apprenticeships to qualify for blue-collar and inferior white-collar jobs while still attending compulsory vocational schools a few hours each week. The Volksschule system does not teach higher mathematics, physics, or chemistry. Foreign language instruction is very limited. Its graduates are automatically barred from the middle and upper-level civil service, from becoming military officers, from most managerial and executive jobs, and the professions. They cannot enter universities or colleges unless they take the long, hard road of adult evening education to qualify for admission.

The remaining 34 per cent—theoretically the most gifted, but all too often the more privileged children of the middle and upper-middle classes—attend either a *Realschule* or *Gymnasium* from which they can be graduated, respectively, at age sixteen or nineteen with certificates equal to or better than American high school diplomas. To qualify for admission to either of these two types of schools, they must pass nationwide exams given at age ten in the fourth grade. The exam is staged only once each year and there is no second chance to take it if the child fails to pass.

Of this select group, half—or about 17 per cent of any year's crop of fifth graders—enter the Realschule system. If they manage to graduate at the end of the tenth grade they receive a certificate equal to a US high school diploma. It is still not good enough for college entry, a professional career, or a commission in the army, but it does give these youths a fighting chance for junior managerial jobs and middle-level civil service posts.

Only the elite—the other 17 per cent—enter a Gymnasium, completion of which at age nineteen results in an *Abitur* degree. To obtain an Abitur certificate—equal to two years of American university education—students must pass stiff oral and written examinations, usually lasting several weeks and given on a statewide basis. The exam is so tough and standards in these schools so high (five to six years of Latin, five years of English, and four or five of French being par for the course) that only half of those who enter a Gymnasium graduate with an Abitur diploma. That diploma is the entrance ticket to the professions, top managerial positions, commissions in the military, and senior civil service jobs. Without an Abitur no German can enter college or university (where they will study from five to eight more years), though under present crowded conditions having an Abi, as kids call it, is no guarantee for acceptance since there is space for only about one-fourth of the Gymnasium graduates.

When it was introduced more than 150 years ago, the Gymnasium system was regarded as a landmark of progress in education. But over the years it has become more and more a preserve of social and political conservatism and of the moneyed elite.

A number of reform proposals were introduced in 1968 and 1969 but it is expected to be 1980 before they are adopted in most of the states. All are based on recognition of the fact that a solid education is no longer a privilege but a right and necessity for all. The proposals acknowledge that an upper school system which filters out the majority of children in the fourth grade and entitles them to only nine full years of education is very much out of date. The reform plans also call for changing the basic West German system to an all-day, five days a week school system. At present most children attend only four hours in the mornings for six days a week, with a good four to five hours of homework each day.

Recognizing the weaknesses of the traditional system, East Germany introduced the "unified ten-year polytechnical upper school," patterned after that of the Soviet Union. Except for a greater emphasis on manual training and the fact that younger children are generally not segregated from the older ones in separate buildings, the system also has a lot in common with the American one.

The basic ten-year course is attended by 84 per cent of East German youths—that is, all but a minority who lack the native ability and leave school after the eighth grade to learn trades. Of the 84 per cent who complete the polytechnical upper school, about half continue for another two to three years, usually in the same building, to obtain an Abitur with which they can enter college. But there are other avenues to a university education, including a more flexible adult program and a system of four-year trade or technical schools, graduation from which leads to college admission. The East German tenth grade diploma is probably not equal to an American high school certificate, but the GDR Abitur ranks scholastically with West Germany's and is on a par with two years of US college.

The East German reform is admirable. It has provided youth with greater opportunities and more education than Germans have ever had. But is it a better education they are getting? Schools in the GDR dispense knowledge, certainly, but they do not teach young people to think, to question, to challenge.

There is method behind this madness, for East Germany's rulers do not want to raise a critical new generation but an obedient one. They are using the schools as tools of propaganda and ideological indoctrination. The two Communist youth groups, the Young Pioneers (for ten to fourteen year olds) and the FDJ, Free German Youth organization (for fourteen to twenty-five year olds), are represented with chapters at every school and college. Membership is not mandatory but "desired" and 70 per cent of all young people belong. Social science and civics courses openly attempt to instill in youngsters a "socialist awareness and view of life." Other courses have the same goal, though lesson plans go about achieving it a little less openly.

Textbooks for pupils learning English, for example, are thinly disguised propaganda pamphlets. They portray an England which is neither merry nor old but caught up in daily class warfare, where workers are constantly afraid of losing their jobs, evil landowners oppress poor farmers, money-mad capitalists crush strikes, and the British Communist party is the only hope for salvation.

Teaching materials in ancient and world history courses describe the classical civilizations—Greece and Rome—primarily as dictatorships in which a privileged minority ruled over an enslaved mass. That is true of course. But is Spartacus' short-lived revolt against Rome really worth more attention in a textbook than the long-term influence of Christianity on the Roman empire? The history of Medieval and Renaissance Europe is pictured as a long series of peasants uprisings against feudal lords. Modern history is seen through a red filter of revolution of which Russia's, of course, is the most important. One fifth grade history book, for example, uses a different color ink to emphasize such words as: labor, tools, work, society, industry, agriculture, exploitation, and poverty.

Educational opportunities, like everything else in East German life, are linked to loyalty to the state. Young people who do not toe the political line, who do not learn their Marxism-Leninism or dialectical materialism as well as the Three R's, or who are not active in the FDJ may find themselves barred from college. Those in universities who get bad grades in basic social studies find themselves expelled or deprived of their government scholarships. Pupils learn at an early age that it pays to act enthusiastic and to repeat the political lecture phrases verbatim. They learn hypocrisy: to say one thing but to think another.

As one student put it, "We know exactly what we are supposed to say. Privately we say something else. We learn this ballyhoo by heart and recite it when asked. But that doesn't mean we have to believe it."

On the surface, this system of indoctrination has turned the GDR into a model society.

More than two million young East Germans are members of amateur athletic organizations. Since 1949 East German youths have won more than 1,000 medals at European sports events and nearly 700 in world championship meets. In the last four Olympic games East German athletes walked off triumphantly with 159 medals, among them 44 in gold—a record topped only by the United States and the Soviet Union, both countries more than ten times as big as the GDR. The ultraconservative London *Times* writes enthusiastically about "the golden age of East German sports" and the regime, very much aware of the value of its young athletes, spends millions of dollars annually to train and provide them with a life more privileged than that of some of the highest paid professionals in the West. "Sports," says Erich Honecker, "is not an end in itself but a means to an end. Our athletes are diplomats and salesmen of socialism in sweatsuits." To make sure it will always have enough of them, the GDR builds 90 million marks' worth of athletic facilities each year.

More than 20 per cent of all new patents in the GDR are registered by *"Meister von Morgen"* (Mastercraftsmen of Tomorrow). These are all young people under twenty-one, some only pupils and apprentices. The GDR has more than 12,000 youth brigades. These are teams of young workers and volunteers who build power plants, dams, highways, and airport runways.

It is a picture that cheers many of the older generation —in both Germanys, one might add. It swells the chests of those elderly Germans who still believe children should be seen, not heard; who consider obedience a citizen's first duty to the state; who look back nostalgically on the clean-cut Hitler Youths who sang and marched for the greater glory of the Reich. What a healthy contrast, they say, to the large number of unwashed, long-haired, pot-smoking, rock-playing West Germans who seem to want to drop out from society. But is it really such a contrast and is it all that healthy?

There must be a reason for the fact that the juvenile delinquency rate is proportionally almost twice as high in the GDR as it is in the Federal Republic. Of all persons charged with crimes, 30 per cent in East Germany are fourteen to twenty-one years old. In the West the same age group accounts for only 18 per cent of those indicted.

In most West German cities and towns you will see defiant, cocky teenagers slouching on street corners, hands balled in their pockets, cigarettes drooping from the corners of their mouths. To impress their girlfriends, boys drag-race jalopies or test their motorbikes for screech volume. Behind the official propaganda façade you will see similar young people in East Germany. The hair may not be quite as long, the clothes not quite as colorful, for the People's Police are watchful guardians of public morality. Nor do they have jalopies, as even the oldest car is still a luxury in the GDR. But they do have motorbikes and when revved up they will roar just as loudly.

On the whole, things are more alike then they are different. Only sometimes they are called by different names. Thus when a seventeen-year-old Bavarian visited his sixteen-year-old cousin in a small city in Thuringia in the summer of 1973, the East German took the West German to the town's only discotheque. The rock group playing was called The Flamingos. The name of the place: The Karl Marx Club.

In West Germany many young people are searching for something. They reject a society whose only value seems to be consumption and more consumption. As one twenty-five-year-old college dropout now living in a Bavarian commune explained, "All my life I heard my parents tell me how hungry and deprived they were during and after the war, and how lucky I was to have everything. And all the time they kept buying and buying and eating and eating. It didn't make sense. I wanted to experience hunger and

*East German teen-agers are much
like their counterparts in the West.*

deprivation too. That's why I moved here where I'm seeking a purpose in life."

They are critical, these young West Germans, especially the college students. They are critical of their own government and just about everyone else's. They ally themselves with American Blacks and Indians, with South American guerillas, and with the rebels in Angola. During the Vietnam War they sided with the Vietcong and they hit the streets in protest when the generals took power in Chile in 1973.

They are anti-establishment. They will tell you, as did Fritz Teufel, a twenty-four-year-old West Berlin student on trial for throwing rocks at a policeman during a demonstration, "It is easier to push a cow through a keyhole than to get one German civil servant to doubt the words of another German civil servant."

They stage sit-ins, teach-ins, and demonstrations. They occupy empty old apartment houses desperately needed for housing to prevent them from being condemned and torn down by real estate speculators who want to build profitable office blocks. They consider their teachers "authoritarian knuckleheads" and demand a voice in the running of their universities. They reject the traditional role of the German professor, a man so exalted and powerful that he has more authority over his teaching assistants and graduate students than most kings have over their subjects.

They are concerned. About pollution of the environment, overpopulation, discrimination against Germany's 2.5 million foreign workers, and about the general direction their society is taking.

In all this they are different from young East Germans, for they have a choice. East German youths also demonstrate—for the government, not against it. They have no choice. The last flicker of rebellion in the GDR was in 1968 when a handful of East Germans protested the invasion of Czechoslovakia by Soviet and East German troops. By Western standards it was not much of a demonstration. In all East Germany no more than 300 people were involved. A few handbills were passed out secretly on street corners in a few cities. A slogan was painted on a wall here, a sidewalk there: "Long Live Dubcek." "Get Out of Prague." "Hands Off Czechoslovakia." The protesters were teenagers and students in their early twenties. The penalties for some were so severe—up to eight years in prison—that I know of no young East Germans who have dared to demonstrate since then. And who can blame them?

10
Two States of Mind

Browsing through a bookshop in Bonn some years ago, I noticed a new paperback by a group of West German journalists about life in the GDR. It had a provocative title: *Journey to a Faraway Land.*

Have the two Germanys, I asked myself, really grown that far apart? There is no easy answer to the question.

I know some West Germans who will tell you, "East Germans seem more foreign to me than Frenchmen do."

Official statistics show that nearly 20 per cent of all West Germans still have family ties with inhabitants of the GDR. But those ties, despite the relaxation of travel restrictions since 1972, seem to grow looser from year to year. Even people who visit each other regularly remark, "we have less in common and less to say to each other each time."

Most West Germans know so little about the GDR that in a recent survey less than 10 per cent were able to say with reasonable accuracy how many people live in East Germany and only 6 per cent recognized the name of the GDR's prime minister.

A number of years ago a language professor at East Berlin's Humboldt University predicted that the day was not far off when shop windows in other countries might display signs reading, "East and West German spoken here." And he was perfectly serious.

So was *Freiheit,* the daily Socialist Unity party paper for the city of Halle, which maintains that "the social development of the GDR and West Germany have taken so different a course over the years that a unified German national language no longer exists."

It is not quite that bad yet. But thanks to the influx of Communist gobbledegook in the East and the popularity of Americanisms in the West, a sort of East-speak and West-speak German has evolved. Already there are striking differences between the eastern and western versions of the *Duden,* the German *Webster's Dictionary.* In the most recent editions more than four hundred words do not appear in one or the other and the two books disagree on definitions for two hundred words.

What, for example, does an East German mean when he talks about the "normative coefficient of the effectiveness of capital investition"? Interest rate, naturally. Who in West Germany would know that an "honored physician of the people" is an ordinary doctor who has received a medal, or that a "hero of socialist labor" is an assembly line worker who produced "above the norm"?

Even swear words seem to have changed their meaning. You can call an East German many things that you could

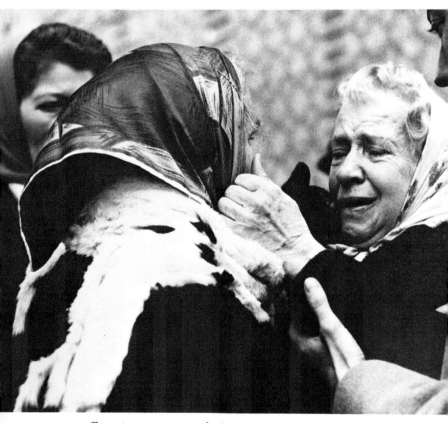

*Two sisters are reunited after
the strain of a long separation.*

not call a West German. But to label him a "subjectivist,"
"reconciliationist" or "capitulant" is the height of insult. The
average West German, however, would not even know what
you meant.

West-speak German on the other hand is a language
laced with English and American expressions, most of them
derived from advertising. These have influenced the language in West Germany far more than Russian has in East
Germany. In fact, says the Bonn Ministry of Intra-German
Affairs, these "Anglo-Americanisms seem to be becoming
increasingly popular in East Germany, too." Bonn officials
regard this as a sign that the two Germanys still have a
great deal in common. So, apparently, do East German
officials who are quite worried about the trend.

"We find it strange," complained *Neue Deutsche Presse,*
the official trade paper of East German journalism, "that
some of our local dailies will praise the socialist way of life
on their front pages while running advertisements inside
which encourage people to buy *party grills, hobby sets,* and
sunshine lotions. Why, when describing the home life and
personal habits of a hero of socialist labor, do they report
that he prefers *Oxford* shirts, usually has a *whisky and soda*
before dinner, and for their anniversary gave his wife a
wristwatch that was trade-named *Darling?*" The words in
italics appeared in the German newspaper text in the original English.

One reason may be that so many East Germans watch
West German television.

"Much has been written about the difficulty of crossing
the wall, but any electron jumps it with ease." So says
Stefan Heym, one of the GDR's best and most outspoken
novelists, who also lived in the US from 1935 to 1952 and

served as an American army officer. "Western radio broadcasts reach everywhere, and western TV can be clearly received in all but two districts. Today the brand names and
advertising slogans of certain West German products have
become household words in the East as well. Films shown
by West German TV are matters of public discussion on
East German trains and streetcars."

Nor should one forget the fact that the two Germanys
are still major trading partners. Interzonal trade, as it is
still called although the occupation zones ceased to exist
long ago, comes to a two-way volume of almost $2.5 billion
a year. Each Germany is the other's second biggest trading
partner, right after the United States (for the FRG) and
Russia (for the GDR). And a very privileged trade it is,
for being considered intra-German, it is free of duties and
taxes.

For many years after division, especially in the 1960s,
East Germany emphasized its Germanness, and in fact,
claimed to be the "better Germany." It identified itself with
all of German history and culture that was good and tried
to shove responsibility for Germany's seedier eras and
heroes off on the Federal Republic. It contended that it
was the "true German fatherland" in a social and historic
sense, a fatherland in which "the rich have been expropri-
ated and deprived of power, a fatherland which has nothing
in common with that of Hindenburg, Krupp, or Eichmann."

Walter Ulbricht used to say, "One should never forget
that Germany has two cultures and two traditions. One is
the nonculture and barbaric tradition of German imperial-
ism which expressed itself in the slaughter of millions at
Auschwitz and today raises its ugly head in support of
American aggression. . . . The other culture is the pro-

gressive tradition of the German nation and its humanistic heritage, represented by the forces of the working people in the GDR. . . ."

And the GDR claimed for itself all those figures of the German past that it considered part of that humanistic heritage. The great writers Johann Wolfgang von Goethe and Friedrich von Schiller may have been born and raised in what is now West Germany, but they did most of their writing in Thuringia, and the GDR wasted no time claiming them as her own. "Hadn't you heard," said one East German writer who disapproved of this sort of historic piracy, "that Schiller became a citizen of the GDR when he settled in Jena in 1789?" The composers Bach, Handel, Schumann, and Wagner were all born in what is now East Germany, and the GDR of course staked a claim on them. Even Martin Luther, Thuringia's most prodigal son, was taken into the fold of what is, officially at least, an atheistic Communist state. For the purpose of the 450th anniversary of the Reformation Luther was portrayed as a German national hero, a progressive force, a forerunner of socialism, as a kind of spiritual godfather of the GDR.

The East German attitude toward the heritage of Prussia was no less opportunistic. Just as in the case of Protestantism, the GDR was fortunate enough to have the meccas of Prussianism within its own borders. The heart of Berlin, at least its historic heart, is in the eastern sector of the city on Unter den Linden avenue, and nearly all the buildings have been meticulously restored and preserved.

But in 1972 the pendulum began to swing in the other direction as the new leadership under Erich Honecker attempted to de-Germanize the GDR and erase as many reminders of the common past as possible. Wherever possible the Honecker regime has obliterated references to "Germany." Radio Germany, the principal broadcasting network, was renamed Voice of the GDR. The Association of German Journalists became known as the Association of Journalists of the GDR. The ten pfenning coins were recalled because they had the word Germany on them. Effective in 1974, the nationality stickers on automobiles had to be changed from the traditional "D," which stood for Deutschland, to "DDR," meaning Deutsche Demokratische Republic. Even the national anthem was no longer being sung, only hummed or played, because there is a passage in it that refers to "Germany, our united Fatherland."

History books were rewritten and lesson plans changed so that school children now learn almost nothing about German history. An attempt is being made to stake out a separate historical identity and the idea seems to be that by dropping all references to "German" and "Germany," people could be induced to forget the common origins of the two countries. This policy is called "demarcation" and one joke making the rounds was that Honecker, just to be safe, wanted to drop the G from the nation's initials and enter the United Nations with a country known only as the DR —the Democratic Republic.

What was behind this sudden shift in policy? Nothing less than the improvement in relations between the two Germanys that followed the signing of the basic treaty between them.

From the outset of his administration Willy Brandt had maintained that there was only one way to save anything of German unity. That was to recognize that there were now two German states but to insist that there could be only "one German nation." By ending the cold war, by recognizing the existence of the GDR, by treating it as an

East German premier Willi Stoph (left) meets West German chancellor Willy Brandt for a round of summit talks.

equal and mature state, Brandt argued, there might be a chance to reweave some of the ties that had been broken by two decades of propaganda and confrontation. Relations between those two states might never be good. But that he insisted "is still an improvement over the situation in which we have no relations at all."

While it is true that the Germanys had no official relations, a relationship of a particular kind has long existed: espionage and counter-espionage.

Günter Guillaume, the East German agent uncovered in Brandt's West German chancellory, is but one of an estimated 8,000 GDR spies believed to be working in West Germany. And according to Günter Nollau, the head of West Germany's chief security and counterintelligence bureau, there must be scores if not hundreds of them who are as highly placed and close to the center of power as Guillaume was. The problem is to uncover them.

This is not to say that West Germany doesn't spy on East Germany. Whenever exchanges of agents who have been caught take place on the border—a clandestine trade that goes on all the time—it is usually the GDR which has more West German "heads" to offer the FRG than vice versa.

This secret war between the two Germanys, rougher and more free-wheeling than between any other two states, is certain to continue. As Erich Honecker put it coldly following Guillaume's arrest: "There is nothing in the basic treaty or the other agreements between the two German states which precludes intelligence operations by either side."

Nevertheless, the basic treaty and the other agreements negotiated by Brandt have provided for more free communication between Germans on both sides of the border than at any time since the building of the Berlin Wall in 1961. Though East Germans are still walled up, the border has become incredibly porous in at least one direction—from West to East. Between Easter 1972 and the fall of 1973 there were more than 7 million visits by West Germans and West Berliners to the GDR and East Berlin.

To Honecker this posed a challenge and he responded by battening down the ideological hatches.

Was it necessary? Is the allure of the West still so great and the East German regime still so unstable that it has to fence itself in even if it can no longer keep westerners out? I cannot answer with certainty, but my impression, and that of thinking East Germans like Stefan Heym, for example, is that the answer is "No."

The standard of living in East Germany has improved so dramatically in recent years that fewer and fewer East Germans are attracted by the sparkle of the West. If they continue to flee—and the rate has increased since the beginning of 1973—then it is for a different reason: People do not want to be fenced in.

"I wouldn't dream of defecting," says one East Berliner. "I've got a comfortable life and security here. All I demand is to be treated like an adult by this regime and to be free to go to West Germany or France or Italy on a vacation."

Or as one East German doctor told me a few years after the wall was first built, "Now that it is there and I can no longer travel back and forth the way I used to, I'd try walking across the border barefoot to get out of here. But if the wall came down I'd stay here, of course. I'd be free to come and go then, wouldn't I?"

The irony is that the East German regime is so unsure of itself and so unable to forget the trauma of the pre-wall exodus that it is afraid to relax travel restrictions. It points to the escapees as proof for the wisdom of its policy. Yet it is the existence of the wall and the restrictions that drive people to risk their lives to escape.

West Germany's strongest appeal today is to a group of East Germans who represent a tiny minority within their own country—liberal Communists, veteran Social Democrats, and left-wing intellectuals who are attracted by the existence of a Social Democratic government in the Federal Republic. These are the same people who for nearly a quarter of a century have been looking for a "third road" to socialism and opposed the orthodoxy of Ulbricht's kind of communism. To them the political changes that have taken place in West Germany represent a great hope. They dream of a freer, more liberal, really democratic East Germany But like their soulmates in all other Communist countries, the tide of history seems to be moving against them. They remember only too well that there was one such an attempt to combine communism with genuine democracy—in Czechoslovakia in 1968. The Soviet Union crushed it with tanks and guns.

Although Brandt's policy brought Germans closer together than at any time in the previous two decades, can the policy he initiated also lead to eventual reunification? The constitutions of both Germanys are still committed to that goal and Brandt's successor, Helmut Schmidt, said upon taking office that it remains his ultimate aim. But with each passing day the prospects seem more remote. Most Germans realize it too. A decade ago, nearly 50 per cent of West Germany's population thought there was a chance; today, those who see it as a possibility represent less than 9 per cent, most of them over fifty.

Of course nothing in politics is ever impossible, and it would be foolish to look too far ahead. Who says that some day there may not be a strong man in either Germany who

Willy Brandt greets Helmut Schmidt,
his successor as chancellor of West Germany.

will come to power on a promise to reunite the two Germanys by force? Romantic nationalism may be a dead issue for young East and West Germans today, but there is no guarantee that it will not grip their children or grandchildren some day. Indeed a warning to that effect has been sounded by some East German Communist intellectuals who say that unless East Germans are allowed to explore their history and culture more honestly, a heavy price could eventually be paid in a reawakening of German nationalism.

But for the forseeable future it seems, for at least as long as the present generation of young East and West Germans dominates the scene, there will be two Germanys.

"We think," says Erich Honecker, "that this is an advantage to the world—to see two independent sovereign states on German soil."

"And we," says a prominent West German politician, "can only hope that in the not too distant future, relations between them will be like those between other independent, sovereign states; that the wall will disappear; that the boundary between them becomes like our border to Austria, Switzerland, France, Belgium, Holland, or Denmark; like East Germany's own border to Poland or Czechoslovakia—with movement of peoples in both directions: free movement. When that happens both Germanys will be truly sovereign and independent."

And unity or division will not really matter any more.

Appendix : A Note About Money

What is a mark? A few years ago when one US dollar equaled four Deutsche marks, the answer to that question was easy. But since 1972, as a result of the international currency crises, the West German mark has been floating. That means its value changes with demand and supply, with the weakness or strength of the American dollar. For that reason most money figures in this book have been given in marks.

Establishing the value of the East German mark is even more difficult because it is not a freely convertible currency. Under East German law it is a serious crime to take East German marks out of the country or to bring them in. At the borders and in all international financial dealings, the East German government rates its mark equal to that of

West Germany, that is, one to one. For the sake of comparison that exchange rate has been used throughout the text. But it is important to know that on the free money markets in Western Europe and West Germany, the value of the East mark changes and has been as low as onefourth of the West mark. People willing to take the risk could buy East German marks cheaply at a West German bank and take them into the country. But if caught it means a severe prison term.

Since the West German mark began floating in its relationship to the American dollar, the East German mark has floated too. American tourists traveling to East Germany generally get as many GDR marks for their dollar as they get FRG marks in West Germany.

Recommended Readings

Prewar and Wartime Germany:
Bullock, Alan, *Hitler, A Study in Tyranny.* New York, Harper & Bros., 1953, revised 1969.
Friedrich, Otto, *Before the Deluge, A Portrait of Berlin in the 1920s.* New York, Harper & Row, 1972.
Hanfstaengl, Ernst, *Unheard Witness.* Philadelphia, J.B. Lippincott, 1957.
Kogon, Egon, *The Theory and Practice of Hell.* New York, Farrar, Straus and Cudahy, 1950.
Kohn, Hans, *The Mind of Germany.* New York, Charles Scribner's Sons, 1960.
Mann, Golo, *The History of Germany Since 1789.* New York, Praeger, 1968.

Payne, Robert, *The Life and Death of Adolf Hitler*. New York, Praeger, 1973.

Reitlinger, Gerald, *The Final Solution*. New York, Beechhurst Press, 1953.

Ryan, Cornelius, *The Last Battle*. New York, Simon and Schuster, 1966.

Shirer, William L., *Berlin Diary*. New York, Alfred A. Knopf, 1941.

Shirer, William L., *The Rise and Fall of the Third Reich*. New York, Simon and Schuster, 1959.

Tuchman, Barbara, *The Guns of August*. New York, Macmillan, 1962.

Wiesenthal, Simon, *The Murderers Among Us*. New York, McGraw-Hill, 1967.

The Cold War and Germany's Division

Barnet, Richard and Raskin, Marcus, *After 20 Years— Alternatives to the Cold War in Europe*. New York, Random House, 1966.

Dulles, Eleanor Lansing, *Berlin—The Wall is Not Forever*. Chapel Hill, N.C., University of North Carolina Press, 1967.

Fleming, D.F., *The Cold War and Its Origins*. New York, Doubleday, 1961.

Horowitz, David, *The Free World Colossus*. New York, Hill & Wang, 1965.

McInnis, Edgar, Hiscocks, Richard, and Spencer, Robert, *The Shaping of Postwar Germany*. Toronto, J.M. Dent & Sons, 1960.

West Germany

Dornberg, John, *Schizophrenic Germany*. New York, Macmillan, 1961.

Elon, Amos, *Journey to a Haunted Land.* New York, Holt, Rinehart & Winston, 1966.
Harpprecht, Klaus, *Willy Brandt.* New York, Abelard-Schuman, 1972.
Leonhardt, Rudolf Walter, *This Germany.* New York, New York Graphic Society, 1964.
Prittie, Terence, *Adenauer: A Study in Fortitude.* Chicago, Henry Regnery, 1972.
Schalk, Adolph, *The Germans.* New York, McGraw-Hill, 1972.
Temple, Gudrun, *The Germans: An Indictment of My People.* New York, Random House, 1963.

East Germany
Dornberg, John, *The Other Germany.* New York, Doubleday, 1968.
Hangen, Welles, *The Muted Revolution.* New York, Alfred A. Knopf, 1966.
Leonhard, Wolfgang, *Child of the Revolution.* Chicago, Henry Regnery, 1959.
Lippmann, Heinz, *Honecker and the New Politics of Europe.* New York, Macmillan, 1972.
Shrader, Herbert L., *No Other Way—The True Story of an East German Surgeon's Escape to the West.* New York, David McKay, 1964.
Smith, Jean, *Germany Beyond the Wall.* Boston, Little, Brown, 1969.
Stern, Carola, *Ulbricht: A Political Biography.* New York, Praeger, 1965.
Wechsberg, Joseph, *Journey Through the Land of Eloquent Silence.* Boston, Little, Brown, 1964.

Index

Index

Photographs appear courtesy of:

John Dornberg: 149 (bottom), 158 (top), 169, 189
Eastfoto: 92, 117, 144
German Information Center: 99, 106, 130, 149 (top),
    158 (bottom), 166, 194
United Press International: 125, 203
Wide World Photos: 21, 26, 47, 55, 60, 71, 79, 86, 179, 199

Maps by David Lindroth